The Road Across Canada

The Road Across Canada

EDWARD McCOURT

Illustrated by
John A. Hall

1965

MACMILLAN OF CANADA

TORONTO

ISBN   7705-0856-1

Library of Congress Catalogue Card No. 65-17065

First printed March 1965
Reprinted October 1965
This edition 1972

Printed in Canada
for the Macmillan Company of Canada Limited
70 Bond Street, Toronto 2

Contents

FOR MARGARET

best of travelling companions

Foreword

This book is the outcome of a journey my wife and I made across Canada on the Trans-Canada Highway in the summer of 1963. It is not a guidebook nor a story of road-building; rather, it is a highly personal impression of things we saw, heard, suffered, and enjoyed in the course of our wanderings between St. John's, Newfoundland, and Victoria, British Columbia.

It is not possible to thank all the people whose kindness helped to make the journey one of the most satisfying and memorable experiences of our lives; but I would like to acknowledge with a special word of gratitude the names of those who assisted us in a practical way: Mr. Dan Wallace and Mr. A. J. Carman, Canadian Government Travel Bureau, Ottawa; Mr. E. J. Marten, Department of Public Works, Ottawa; Miss Jessie Mifflen, Chief Regional Librarian, St. John's, Newfoundland (who welcomed us mainlanders and placed her excellent CBC talks on off-beat aspects of Newfoundland life at my disposal); Miss Marjorie Mews, Gosling Memorial Library, St. John's; Miss Hazel Macdonald, Sydney, Nova Scotia; Mrs. Sybil MacLean, Montague, Prince Edward Island; Mrs. Wm. Argue, Fredericton, New Brunswick; Miss Margaret Tanner, Department of External Affairs, Ottawa; and Mrs. R. H. Wright of Vancouver.

Finally, my warmest thanks to Mr. John Gray and Mr. Jim Bacque of The Macmillan Company of Canada for encouraging me to write this book the way I wished to write it.

Edward McCourt

Foreword to the Second Edition

Since we first travelled the length of the Trans-Canada Highway in 1963 there have been, inevitably, many changes in the Highway and the world through which it passes. To name only a few: the Newfoundland section of the Highway has long since been completed, and a splendid road it is too; the restoration of Louisbourg fortress has made astonishing progress; up-to-date accommodations and camp-sites have burgeoned the length of the Highway; and, unfortunately, Custer no longer makes his Last Stand over the entrance to the Fort Qu'Appelle Hotel beer parlour. But the grand essentials – the fishing villages and the great cities and the plains and the big sky and the mountains and the oceans which wash our shores – remain unchanged. There is still no better road to an understanding and a love of our land and our people than the Trans-Canada Highway.

Edward McCourt

The Trail-Blazers

In the year 1912 the citizens of the town of Alberni on Vancouver Island, together with 'throngs of public-spirited men and women from Victoria, Vancouver, and Nanaimo', assembled by the roadside on the outskirts of town and set up a signpost bearing an arrow pointing east and the inscription 'Canadian Highway'. The sign marked the beginning – or the end, depending on the direction you looked – of a dream road, the Trans-Canada Highway, first conceived in the mind of Sir James Douglas, Governor of British Columbia, in the mid nineteenth century.

Two nights after the ceremony the citizens of Port Alberni a mile and a half away dug up the signpost and re-erected it within the limits of the Port. It was recovered without bloodshed, restored to its original hole, and guarded for an indefinite period by a husky bull-terrier, 'fierce and aggressive of disposition and sharing the local indignation'. To ensure his unremitting vigilance the bull-terrier was chained to the signpost.

Pessimists viewed the signpost with some scepticism; the more extreme among them ventured to predict (*sotto voce*) that the Highway might not be completed for another twenty or even twenty-five years. The common view settled for ten at the outside. After all, the Canadian Highway Association had been active for more than two years now, and a gentleman of Victoria named Todd had already struck a medal to be awarded to the first Canadian motoring from coast to coast on Canadian roads.

On September 3rd, 1962, exactly half a century after the Alberni sign-planting ceremony, the Trans-Canada Highway was officially declared open. The signpost had long since rotted away.

It had of course been possible for nearly twenty years prior to the official opening to travel from Halifax to Vancouver by an all-Canadian route, but long stretches of loose gravel and narrow, twisting mountain road, particularly around the Big Bend in British Columbia, constituted hazards sufficiently disagreeable and alarming to impel the average motorist to seek the safety and convenience of the excellent U.S. highways adjacent to the border. The Highway opened in 1962 eliminated most of the hazards, drove its way through some of the finest and least familiar scenery on the continent, tied together disparate segments of the sprawling Dominion, and satisfied national pride. No doubt we on this continent have always tended to exaggerate the importance of mere size; none the less, it is gratifying to know that the 5,000-mile Trans-Canada Highway is the longest continuous road on earth.

Although it was not until after the Second World War that Canadians in any number drove from one side of Canada to the other on Canadian roads, there were inevitably those daring adventurers who attempted the crossing in the days when the automobile, like many of the roads it rattled over, was untried, unpredictable, badly serviced, and subject under pressure to complete collapse. The first of these overland Columbuses to leave a record of his journeyings in the days when roads beyond long-settled areas were seldom more than wandering trails was an excellent Englishman, Thomas Wilby, who in the year 1912 covered the distance from Halifax to Victoria in just under two months. Wilby's book, *A Motor Tour Through Canada*, is fortunately much more than an account of the hazards of motoring in Canada half a century ago – it is also an acute commentary on Canadian ways of life and a fascinating revelation of a personality compounded in almost equal proportions of adventurer, sociologist, and poet.

Wilby, after dipping the wheels of his car in the Atlantic and offering appropriate libations to St. Christopher, left Halifax on August 20th, 1912, and headed in the general direction of the Pacific. His late-model, high-riding car was a portable garage; the equipment hanging over the sides or stowed away in odd corners, running-board boxes, and rear-end trunks included spare motor

parts, spare tires, cans of oil and gas, axes, shovels, and – most useful
of all – a heavy block-and-tackle. With only a few minor deviations
and no trouble whatever Wilby followed the route of the present
Trans-Canada Highway through the Maritimes and into Quebec.
In Quebec City he met his first check – the heavily burdened car
balked at the steep climb into the Upper Town. Wilby – red-faced,
sweating, hideously embarrassed – instructed his pilot-driver to back
up the hill. Then he basely abandoned driver and car and, pretend-
ing to be an interested spectator, mingled with the cheering crowd
that lined the street. The experience was instructive as well as embarrassing. Thereafter whenever a steep slope loomed ahead Wilby
put his faith in the all-powerful reverse gear. Indeed there are times
when his narrative suggests that he drove across Canada backwards.

Wilby followed uncertain trails along the St. Lawrence to Montreal, then drove to Ottawa and thence to Toronto via Kingston over
excellent roads. But the run from Toronto to North Bay, which occupied nearly two weeks, proved a nightmare experience – the worst
of the entire trip. Wilby's view of the country through which he
travelled is neatly summarized in his description of a hamlet called
Scotia Junction, about seventy miles from North Bay, where he was
delayed several days waiting for a new drive-shaft to be shipped
from Toronto:

'Scotia Junction was a geographical expression set down promis-
cuously and irrelevantly in a swamp in the heart of Ontario. It was
a fitting spot in which to hide effectively the ignominy of disaster;
but one would have preferred companionship in congested ways,
or the enchantment of the broad St. Lawrence or the roar of bel-
ligerent seas – anything but this Sibyl silence of dreary flats, a hush
broken only by the raucous grinding of metallic wheels and the
wheezing cough of aggressive locomotives.'

Somewhere in the lonely desolation between Scotia Junction and
North Bay Wilby threw away his hitherto precious sheet of printed
road instructions. 'Roads were mentioned in them which no On-
tarian wiseacre or compass could locate, though eager search was
made for them – for anything, in fact, rather than the ways of sand
and swamp and oleaginous pools which now began to mark our
progress.'

Victoria Vancouver Fraser Canyon Kamloops Banff Calgary

BRITISH COLUMBIA   ALBERTA

'Progress' to North Bay involved bouncing over primitive corduroy roads through dismal mosquito-haunted swamps, bridging a creek with materials borrowed from a near-by farm, and surmounting innumerable sand-ridden, virtually trackless hills with the aid of jack, block-and-tackle, reverse gear, and sheer muscle-power. Why Wilby didn't suffer a heart attack or at the very least a hernia must forever remain a mystery.

North Bay marked the end of the first stretch of continuous road and trail. The way north-west to Sudbury lay through trackless forest. Wilby took a train to Sudbury and from there was able to drive as far as Sault Ste. Marie. Between Sault Ste. Marie and Winnipeg lay nearly a thousand miles of rock and swamp and forest unmarked by any trails except those cut by lumbermen. But Wilby, a stout Empire man, refused to consider crossing the border and profaning his wheels by the touch of American soil. Instead he shipped across Lake Superior to Port Arthur, travelled by rail to Winnipeg, and from Winnipeg struck off across the prairies.

His reaction to the prairies after emerging from the rock and forest of the Laurentian Shield was one of disappointment. He found the landscape dull and featureless — 'a great untimbered dried-up sea of land'. And the roads baffled him. Especially in Saskatchewan, where not even a succession of pilot-drivers, all allegedly familiar with the trails and terrain, could keep him headed due west for any length of time. The Western municipal system of sectional roads looked fine on the map, but the map was prophetic rather than realistic — the system existed only in well-settled areas. Between such areas Wilby followed trails which often petered out in a farmyard or a slough. On such occasions he simply struck out across the unfenced, trackless

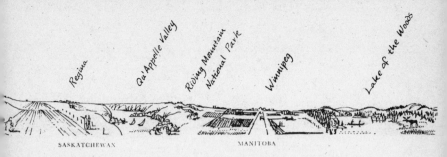

Regina   Qu'Appelle Valley   Riding Mountain National Park   Winnipeg   Lake of the Woods

SASKATCHEWAN   MANITOBA

prairie, guided by his compass and sometimes the stars.

These 'rudderless wanderings' were complicated by rain, gumbo, mosquitoes, and uncomfortable lodgings. But Wilby endured his tribulations with urbane good humour, and as he pushed his way farther west found his feelings about the prairie undergoing a profound change. The poet in him responded instinctively to the colour, the solitude, the mystery of the surrounding immensity. The country bordering the Cypress Hills between Maple Creek and Medicine Hat moved him to his most lyrical outburst:

'The day was superb. A rim of purple hills rimmed the West and flanked us on both sides. Little white houses with red tops stood out here and there against the blue sky. A long train snaked a line of black across the pinkish earth, and occasionally a badger peeped out of his yawning and dangerous burrow in the dim roadway. . . . In the short grass we found the ineffaceable eternal trail of the departed monarch – a dark brown line a foot or so wide, running parallel north to south. . . . Pencil lines in the vastness of the country, but their very persistence seemed to prove the reality of the Red Man's dream of the buffalo's return.'

Reflecting with awe and gratification on the contrast between modern, comfortable, high-speed locomotion and the tedium of travel in Red River cart and prairie schooner, Wilby hurtled out of Fort Macleod towards the great barrier of the Rockies at twenty-five miles an hour. He surmounted the Crowsnest Pass with comparative ease, backed into British Columbia, dropped down to Cranbrook and on over an appalling swamp-and-mountain trail to Yak, just inside the Canadian border. No trails of any kind led west from Yak, but Wilby was undismayed; he mounted his car on

5

the railway track and made a night run on the ties to Creston, fourteen miles west. He acknowledges that the run was a bit hard on the nerves since he had no authorization to use the track and no guarantee of clearance. But the personal danger, he assures us, was minimal, since he and his passenger, a fellow Englishman from Cranbrook who had gone along just for the ride, kept a keen look-out and were ready to leap for life at sight of a headlight.

The rest of the journey was a series of mad wanderings over mountain and through swamp, relieved by occasional short rail trips in areas where no track of any kind existed. But no matter how primitive the regions into which he strayed, Wilby — true-blue Englishman to the core — nearly always found solace after the heat and labour of the day in a 'club' of some sort (perhaps he organized it on the spot) where over a glass of appropriate refreshment he chatted with the locals and stored up impressions of the native character. These impressions he communicates to his readers with wit and discernment and sometimes genuine lyrical passion. Witness his comparison between the settled conservative Maritimer, rooted in the good earth, asking little of life beyond reasonable subsistence, and 'the owners of the West, who will let neither mountain nor prairie sleep; who are alive with fundamental action, who cannot rest, who cannot wait . . .'.

Near Ashcroft, the jumping-off place for the Cariboo gold-fields, Wilby witnessed a meeting between old and new that was a symbolic forecast of the triumph of efficiency over romance: 'A number of wagons with long spans of horses were pulling out of town, moving slowly up the winding road. They formed one of the picturesque freight caravans which for years . . . have plied along the

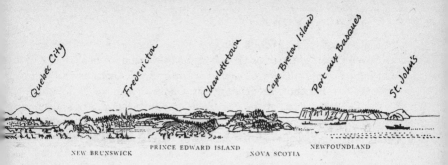

NEW BRUNSWICK PRINCE EDWARD ISLAND NEWFOUNDLAND
      NOVA SCOTIA

Cariboo Trail between Ashcroft and the gold district of Soda Creek and Barkerville. Shooting past them hurried the automobile "stage", a huge red-painted affair, great of horse-power, which of late has disputed service on the Cariboo Trail.'

The teamsters impressed Wilby more than the stage-driver did; they were 'men huge of limb and arm, big of head and broad of shoulder, and generally of that splendid physique which stoically bears hardship, while it inspires the puny denizen of the city with a frantic desire to revise anatomical lines and be born again.'

Wilby's chief assistant in his mountain wanderings was an un-named relief driver whom he picked up somewhere in Saskatchewan. The relief driver had difficulty disposing his excessively long limbs inside the crowded car and seems to have been at his happiest and most useful lying full length on a fender listening for odd motor noises and effecting necessary adjustments while the car was in full flight. During a night run through the Fraser Canyon the acetylene lamps went out at a point where the road snaked along a terrifying rock-face. But the man from Saskatchewan rose easily to the occasion; he draped himself along a fender, held an oil-lantern low enough to enable Wilby to see the outside edge of the road, and so lighted the car ten miles into Lytton. Even Wilby, to whom hair-raising experiences were by this time a commonplace, acknowledges that the feat was somewhat out of the ordinary.

Fifty-two days out of Halifax Thomas Wilby reached the city of Victoria and there emptied into the Pacific ocean the flask of Atlantic water he had carried with him all the way across Canada.

He assures us that the trip was accomplished 'with the minimum of discomfort'.

7

The Road Across Canada

Eight years after Wilby's odyssey Percy Gomery of Vancouver travelled part of the trans-Canada route by car and wrote a book, *A Motor Scamper 'Cross Canada* — as coy and gelatinous as its title suggests — describing his achievement. Gomery's scamper, being under the sponsorship of the Canada Motor Association, was widely publicized, and branches of the association all across the country stood by to extend appropriate hospitality and aid. The publicity seems hardly warranted since Gomery began his journey at Montreal and basely deserted Canadian soil at Sault Ste. Marie to follow what in 1920 was known as the King's International Highway through Michigan, Wisconsin, and Minnesota. He popped up into Canada again at Emerson, Manitoba, after following U.S. highways for 600 miles. From British Columbia he again dropped down across the border into Washington and followed the familiar U.S. Highway Nos. 2 and 10 over the Snoqualmie Pass and on to the coastal road running north to Vancouver. The trip occupied thirty-two days.

But Gomery deserves praise on two counts: he did all his own driving and he took his wife with him. Mrs. Gomery, referred to as 'the Skipper' — occasionally 'the little woman' — was of a temperament slightly less bland and equable than her husband's. She was never entirely at ease sitting in a rain-swept forest clearing surrounded by mosquitoes, blackflies, and fearsome wild animals while Percy — unruffled, smiling — squelched through a sea of mud to recover a tire-chain lost half a mile back, or a car-top swept off by a low-hanging branch.

Thomas Wilby — lean, tweedy, direct, and passionate — tackled all obstacles head on or backwards; Percy Gomery — rotund, bland, perpetually smiling — advanced on them sideways (except when trapped by a road admitting no deviations). His cunningly oblique approach to life's problems is exemplified in his successful efforts to spare the Skipper — and himself — the horrors of small-town hotel accommodation. Almost invariably he was able to cajole the owners of the most attractive house in town into providing food and lodging: 'The happiest habit we formed was that of forcing our presence for the night on unsuspecting peaceful families. At first the private home was a matter of necessity, but quickly it became a contrived accident, while the hotel was a sheer obligation and a last resort. A

8

solution for it all is camping, but, although the necessity for such an equipment was not overlooked by the Skipper and me, we rarely used it. The truth is that, on a strenuous trip, one does not do anything that he can pay anybody else to do.'

Only in Saskatchewan were the Gomerys compelled to camp – not because of inhospitality but because of sheer distance and bad roads. Night trapped them once, and they pitched their tent on the open prairie. Percy snatched an hour or two of fitful slumber but the Skipper lay awake all night waiting for the wolves to attack. The experience may explain the uncharacteristic vigour and forthrightness of Gomery's comments on the state of Saskatchewan roads. These comments were given wide publicity in all Saskatchewan papers hostile to the provincial government.

In Manitoba Mr. Gomery scampered a little too fast. He was arrested for driving on the King's International Highway at a speed of nearly forty miles an hour.

The most widely publicized of all trans-Canada runs was made in 1925 by Ed Flickenger, a professional photographer who naturally made a pictorial record of his exploit instead of writing a book about it. Flickenger was sponsored by a well-known automobile firm, hence the attendant publicity. He drove from Halifax to Vancouver in forty days, averaging 120 miles a day. Since he stayed inside Canada all the way his feat was hailed as one of 'historical significance'. The truth is, though, that when Flickenger encountered a really serious obstacle – a few hundred miles of trackless forest or an awkward mountain barrier – he resorted to a mode of locomotion which Thomas Wilby and Percy Gomery would have considered beneath contempt; he replaced his conventional car-wheels with a set of specially constructed steel flanges and drove on the railway tracks. Since clearance was always arranged for him well in advance, the eight hundred miles he covered by rail were probably the safest and most comfortable of the entire trip.

Flickenger was not awarded the Todd medal. No doubt the committee in charge felt that a vehicle equipped to travel with equal facility on roads and rails was not an automobile in the true meaning of the word. It was also pointed out that while Flickenger had

undoubtedly driven inside Canada all the way he actually left Canadian *soil* every time he rode on steel.

The Todd medal was finally awarded in 1946, nearly thirty-five
years after it was struck, to Brigadier R. A. Macfarlane who drove
from Louisbourg, Nova Scotia, to Victoria in nine days. By 1946 a
series of paved and gravelled roads formed a continuous highway of
sorts across Canada, and the Brigadier's run was routine. It is fair
to say that he won the medal by default – no one was interested in
competing for it.

The records of the early trail-blazers may be read by the present
generation with astonishment and awe, but their appeal to those of
us who grew up in the day of the high-riding Model T and the rutted
dirt trail is primarily nostalgic. They bring back memories of the
almost-forgotten time when each car was a distinct personality –
perverse, idiosyncratic, lovable, and hateful, like a dog or horse
obedient only to the master familiar with its ways, and responsive to
persuasions (including the occasional well-placed kick) unknown
to the modern mechanic. The time when every car-owner lived on
intimate terms with the good earth – wallowed in the stuff while re-
pairing a flat or hunting a tire-chain lost in a mud-hole, and arrived
home with a substantial acreage clinging to his boots. The time when
he listened with straining ears for an unfamiliar engine cough or
wheeze, tasted the oily tang of gasoline drawn by mouth through a
blocked feed-pipe, stood by a roadside waiting for the farmer's team
to haul him out of a pot-hole, and poured home brew – the original
anti-freeze – into the radiator and draped the hood in horse-blankets
to keep out the winter's chill.

That time is past now. The modern automobile is a tin-sheathed
monster which usually does its job with impersonal efficiency and
when it doesn't is treated by an impersonal service-station man who
knows nothing of barbed-wire improvisations or nutmeg-grater tire-
repair kits or anything of the marvellous first-aid paraphernalia
which every old-time motorist carried as a matter of course in the
tool-box clamped to the running-board.

But we old-timers remember. And herein lies the chief value of the records of the early trail-blazers. They remind us that we too were of an heroic breed and didn't know it.

In 1949 Parliament approved an act authorizing the federal government to enter into a cost-sharing agreement with the provinces for the construction of a first-class paved highway across Canada, 4,876.5 miles in length. The federal government assumed responsibility for roughly 50 per cent of the general costs, and for 100 per cent of the cost of 140 miles of highway through the national parks lying along the route. Adjustments in cost-sharing since the drawing-up of the original agreement have resulted in the federal government's assuming greater responsibility in certain areas.

It must not, however, be assumed that the Trans-Canada Highway is a wholly new road. Rather, it represents improvisation on the grand scale – the incorporating into an over-all design of already-existing provincial highways of the approved standard of excellence, the raising of other provincial roads to the same standard, and the construction of connecting links through parts of the country where previously no roads of any kind had run. Incomprehensibly, most of the already-existing provincial highways incorporated into the grand design have preserved their original numbers; and the traveller who assumes that the Trans-Canada Highway is No. 1 all the way – as of course it should be – is soon disillusioned and probably lost.

Original plans called for the completion of the Highway by 1956, but demands on provincial governments for roads more immediately suitable to the needs of their electorates, and the engineering problems involved in the construction of several of the connecting links – notably along the north shore of Lake Superior and through the Rogers Pass in British Columbia – delayed completion of the project for another six years.

Thirteen years after the passing of the Highway Act the last link through the Rogers Pass between Golden and Revelstoke was completed and an all-Canada highway ran unbroken – except for the brief interventions of two oceans – from St. John's, Newfoundland, to Victoria, British Columbia. On September 3rd, 1962, the official opening took place, appropriately at the head of the Rogers Pass in the heart of the British Columbia Rockies.

Unfortunately the official opening convinced many people that the Highway was completed *according to the original plan*. The truth is that in 1962 hundreds of miles of highway, mostly in Newfoundland, were unpaved and brutally rough, and many of the provincial roads east of the Manitoba border were still in process of being rebuilt in order to bring them up to the required standard. Even now the Highway is complete only in the sense that it is continuous and passable — there are still hundreds of miles of rebuilding and paving to be done.

Over 3,000 people attended the official opening, including the prime minister of Canada, representatives of the provincial governments, and the members of an official motorcade who had driven the Highway from St. John's to Victoria (over a period of two months) and retraced their tracks to the Pass.

The solemnity of the ceremony was from time to time lightened by a few genial evidences of human frailty. The band of the Princess Patricia's Light Infantry arrived on schedule to provide appropriate patriotic music, but the truck carrying the instruments got lost and the band was unable to play 'O Canada'. The speeches ran more than half an hour over the scheduled time, but one or two of them, reversing the usual pattern, made up in interest what they lacked in brevity. The minister of highways from British Columbia, obviously on terms of intimacy with the Almighty rare even among politicians, said, 'I want to thank God *personally* for the beautiful weather He has given us,' and the minister from Saskatchewan, no doubt uneasy away from his native plains and confused by a vertical landscape, expressed his pleasure at being in Quebec.

Happily, someone had remembered to bring a pair of scissors and the Right Honourable John Diefenbaker, Prime Minister of Canada, was able to cut the ribbon and declare the longest continuous road on earth, the Trans-Canada Highway, officially open.

Tide and Wind and Crag

NEWFOUNDLAND

The Highway begins on Signal Hill high above the city of St. John's in Newfoundland. Signal Hill is a good starting-point, for it provides a splendid view of land and ocean and is rich in history. John Cabot, so all loyal Newfoundlanders affirm, entered the narrow-necked harbour below the Hill in 1497; and 500 years earlier Leif Ericsson may have sighted the craggy summit from far out at sea. Here in the autumn of 1762 France made her last stand in America against Great Britain; and nearly 150 years later in a tower on the Hill a young man named Marconi received the first transatlantic wireless signals. The fortifications built during the eighteenth and nineteenth centuries have long since been demolished except for a few guns which point their ancient muzzles towards the harbour entrance, and the summit of the Hill is now a National Historic Park.

We had travelled, my wife and I, nearly 4,000 miles to reach our starting-point, firm in the belief that all true journeys must follow the course of the sun. In the warm morning light the city of St. John's looked exactly as it does in the travel brochures – the harbour lying directly below us, snug, difficult of access, a grey destroyer tied up at dock; the Confederation Building, massive, uninspired, dominating the city by sheer height and weight; Memorial University sprung fully formed from the rocks overnight; the brightly painted, box-shaped houses climbing the steep slopes above Water Street; and beyond the city the great empty land fading westward into a blue haze of distance.

An American girl standing beside us cried out passionately, 'I'm never going to make friends with anyone again. Never! because you have to leave them . . .'

She was an air-force wife on her way from Rhode Island, where she had lived for the past two years, to the great American naval base at Argentia eighty miles from St. John's on the shore of Placentia Bay. Her cry was not one of anger against Newfoundland which she admitted was both hospitable and beautiful; it was the bitter protest of the ordinary human being who seeks to put down roots and cannot, of the reluctant wanderer who can lay no claim to any part of earth except that inalienable heritage of all men – six feet at the end of life.

We drove down Signal Hill and along Water Street – once the dwelling-place of great merchant princes but now a rather shabby late-Victorian shopping thoroughfare where fishermen sell freshly-caught fish out of barrows – and turned down a precipitous side-street to take a last look at the narrow harbour where ships of many nations have anchored for going on 500 years. Here along the water-front you may see brightly uniformed British marines, French and Spanish and Italian sailors, dark men from the East, and Portuguese fishermen wearing gold rings in their ears to protect them from the perils of the deep. (We missed the fishermen here, but later in North Sydney we saw the mother-ship of the Portuguese fleet, the *Gil Eannes*, lying in harbour. A burly man, naked to the waist, sat on deck and played a stringed instrument as brown-skinned, dark-haired sailors sprawled at ease near by and listened. A romantic scene – and it mattered hardly at all that the minstrel's stringed instrument was a banjo and the air he played the 'Beer-barrel Polka'.)

St. John's is old and Water Street the oldest part of it. Some, including Michael Harrington, Newfoundland's unofficial poet laureate, say it is the oldest street in America –

> I was, before Manhattan Isle changed hands,
> Traded for beads and buckles; middle-aged
> When Halifax was pink-cheeked and full-breasted;
> And when proud Rio was a noisome swamp
> Commerce was striking bargains on my docks . . .

When in 1583 Sir Humphrey Gilbert arrived in St. John's to claim Newfoundland for Queen Elizabeth he found no fewer than thirty-six ships – Portuguese, French, Spanish, and English – lying in the harbour. Gilbert pitched his tent on Water Street and strolled its length with the English merchants who were already the acknowledged harbour lords. He drowned on his way back to England, calling out over the tumultuous seas – so his pious biographer, obviously a man of unusual auditory powers, reports – that heaven is as near by water as by land. A modest plaque at the base of the National War Memorial in St. John's commemorates Gilbert as the founder of Britain's overseas empire.

Fire has ravaged St. John's many times, and none of its buildings has survived long enough to acquire an antique patina. Visitors are called upon to admire the Roman Catholic Basilica of St. John the Baptist; the Colonial Building, seat of government from 1850 to 1960; the fine National War Memorial; and an Anglican Cathedral dating in its present form from 1882 and designed by the Sir Gilbert Scott who earlier perpetrated the Albert Memorial and St. Pancras Station. But the city pleases chiefly by composite effect, by the sum of its parts rather than the parts themselves. The steep, twisting streets, the box-like frame houses, and the old brick tenements studded with chimney-pots look foreign – and at a distance exotic – to the eye accustomed to conventional North American town planning and architecture. And, even though it isn't possible to ignore entirely the city slums, it is comforting to know that they are gradually being eliminated and that in the meantime the children who inhabit them are not always confined to mean and narrow streets. For the sea and the great rocky ridges lie all about the city, they penetrate far into it and provide a harsh and magnificent and easily accessible playground.

For the first fifty or sixty miles out of St. John's the Highway crosses a wild moorland of rock and pond and tundra (in Newfoundland any body of water less than a hundred square miles or so in extent is called a pond) – a queer dishevelled region where the Almighty appears to have assembled all the materials essential to a large-scale act of creation and to have quit with the job barely begun. Ponds are dropped indiscriminately in valleys and on hill-tops, rocks strewn

A fishing-port with 'flakes' or platforms for drying cod

everywhere with purposeless prodigality. But presently the Highway pushes into the narrow neck of land joining the Avalon Peninsula to the main body of the island – Trinity Bay on the right-hand side, Placentia (once the domain of France) on the left – and chaos yields to order and design.

No doubt the glimpses of sea and headland and village we catch from the Highway charm us because they are familiar and hence reassuring. We have seen a thousand times in pictures and imagination the long sea-arm thrusting into the land, the precipitous rock-face reaching down to the shore, the fishing boats riding at anchor in the snug harbour, the fish drying on the 'flakes', the brightly painted, box-like houses climbing down the rock-face – some projected on stilts out over the water – and the white church at the centre of things. All these familiar elements are here in the peninsular settlements which the Highway passes – in Chapel Arm and Norman's Cove and Come-by-Chance and La Manche and a score of others.

All these and something more. When Keats wrote his famous lines about magic casements opening on the foam of perilous seas in fairy lands forlorn he wasn't thinking about Newfoundland but I suspect he may have been thinking of a region very much *like* Newfoundland. The light that falls over land and sea softens outlines, diffuses them, invests objects with that indistinct, eerie beauty which the word 'fairyland' connotes. 'Forlorn' with its suggestion of loneliness, of desolation, provides exactly the right balance. Beautiful in sunlight, magical in the soft, rising mists of a summer morning, the Newfoundland coast – even in summer sunlight – hints at a world that must test to the limit the endurance and fidelity of men when the sea runs strong and cold and the wind is bitter and the loneliness and dark close in and there is nothing to feel or know except nature's chill indifference. No doubt men who go down to the sea in ships learn to face danger with a proud unconcern that landlubbers never know, but not even in Newfoundland, so E. J. Pratt persuades us, can stoicism or the fifteenth chapter of 1 Corinthians triumph wholly over the sea's enduring menace:

> It took the sea a thousand years,
> A thousand years to trace
> The granite features of this cliff
> In crag and scarp and base.

> It took the sea an hour one night,
> An hour of storm to place
> The sculpture of these granite seams
> Upon a woman's face.

Our first day out of St. John's we stopped for lunch in a cove-town overlooking a fine, deep harbour. The tiny restaurant was crowded with natives who observed us with no enthusiasm and little interest, their chief concern being a neighbour woman who had just had all her upper teeth pulled and was soothing her bloody cavities with a cone of soft ice-cream. We fell into talk with a man at the table next to ours – the Scottish skipper of a boat taking on lumber in the cove-town to be unloaded in some far-off port. He had already been ashore five days and was the drunkest man I have ever seen in a vertical position. The town, he assured us in a blurred Clydeside accent, left a man no choice at all. Newfoundlanders, he said, had never heard of those other pleasures normally provided for sailors in ports all round the world.

In St. John's a big Irishman had looked at us out of eyes shrouded in a more-than-Celtic melancholy and said, 'For people like you we say special novenas.' Fifty miles out of the city we drove off paved highway onto a rock-and-gravel-surfaced trail and knew what the big Irishman meant. The unpaved sections of the Highway in Newfoundland – in 1963 nearly 400 miles out of a total of 600 – presented us with a wide variety of terrors, some new in our experience, others harking back to the days of the Model T Ford. Rock-fills lightly coated with sand or gravel (the kind of road-bed that keeps a man vibrating steadily for hours after he has stopped driving) ; dense clouds of dust hanging over the road for miles, through which monstrous trucks and cats (lights ablaze and visible through the dust for ten feet) bore down upon us with terrifying speed; roller-coaster forest trails hardly more than one-way tracks; blind hills and paralysing right-angle curves – these were the orthodox hazards of the unpaved sections of the Trans-Canada Highway in Newfoundland.

And, added to these, certain unorthodox hazards arising not from deficiencies in the Highway but from the ordinary Newfoundlander's attitude towards it – hazards which nothing in the mainlander's previous experience has prepared him for.

In Newfoundland the Trans-Canada Highway is a footpath for pedestrians, a livestock run, a parking-lot 600 miles long and thirty feet wide, a playground for children – and lastly a traffic route for motor vehicles.

Even where good shoulders exist Newfoundlanders prefer to park squarely on the pavement – often just around a curve or over the top of a steep hill. *All* male Newfoundlanders fish (a generalization that admits of no exceptions) and any day of the week or hour of the day you must be prepared to find cars parked in rows on the Highway parallel to a near-by fishing stream. And the children, whose numbers bear witness to the potency of fish diet and baby bonuses, find the Highway the one piece of level terrain for miles around – Newfoundland villages don't bother much with such extravagances as sidewalks and conventional street layouts – and make fullest use of it from dawn till dusk.

Fortunately there isn't much livestock in Newfoundland; otherwise the Highway would be impassable.

'A wonderful road,' the truck-driver at the wayside coffee-stop said. 'The lots in St. John's is full of cars folks like you drove over from Port aux Basques and didn't figure was worth driving back. A wonderful wonderful road.'

No irony here, and no paradox. Technically the road we drove over was for two-thirds of its length enough to make mad the guilty and appal the free: an endless succession of iron-surfaced washboard, gaping pot-holes, and naked rock – a shoulder-twisting, neck-snapping, dust-shrouded horror.

But wonderful in that it exists at all.

For the difficulties facing the road-makers are stupendous. The Highway passes through hundreds of miles of virtually unpopulated terrain combining all the most obstructive features of rock and water and muskeg. In places the muskeg must be reamed out to a depth of twenty-five feet or more and rock-filled to create a solid road-bed. The part of the road that runs through Terra Nova National Park, rock-filled nearly all the way, was completed at a cost of just under half a million dollars a mile. That the Highway exists at all in Newfoundland is indeed wonderful; that it is passable all the way is a miracle.

The average Newfoundlander is immensely pleased with his province's section of the Highway but he doesn't think of it as part of something greater – of a unifying thread running from ocean to ocean and binding him closer to his fellow Canadians. He looks upon the Highway as a means of easy access to good fishing spots, a handy pathway between villages previously isolated from one another except perhaps by sea, and a convenient parking-lot. As a link with the mainland it is of no importance whatever.

There is logic in his view since to him the mainland itself is of little or no importance. The Newfoundlander doesn't think of himself as Canadian — and won't for another generation or two. Government subsidies, baby bonuses, the eloquence of Joseph Smallwood, and the presence of a fellow Islander in the National Hockey League have banished the active hostility of a former time; and the New-foundlander no longer sings, as he did in 1867,

> Men hurrah for our own native isle, Newfoundland,
> Not a stranger shall hold one inch of her strand;
> Her face turns to Britain, her back to the Gulf —
> Come near at your peril, Canadian wolf! . . .
>
> Would you barter the rights your fathers have won?
> No! Let them descend from father to son.
> For a few thousand dollars Canadian gold
> Don't let it be said that our birthright was sold!

But England is still at his front door, the eastern States at his back, and he is almost sure to have relatives in Boston. (More Newfound-landers live in Boston than in St. John's.) Saskatchewan, by contrast with England and the eastern States, is as remote and isolated as Samarkand and no more important.

Nor is the average Newfoundlander much interested in the tourists whom the Highway is attracting to the island in ever-increasing numbers. Making money out of visitors is an industry that doesn't appeal to him, and for this indifference those of us fortunate enough to enjoy the warm-hearted, disinterested Newfoundland hospitality still prevalent have reason to be glad. But the tourists are on the march; already accommodation lags behind demand, and the New-foundlanders are a little dismayed by all the fuss and confusion. True, efforts are being made to cope with the influx — boarding-houses transformed overnight into guest homes, motels mushrooming at strategic points along the Highway, and Junior Chamber of Commerce information booths staffed by pretty girls popping up on the outskirts of the larger towns. But the tourist accustomed to orthodox mainland accommodation is likely to be a little shaken by the treatment accorded him in the Newfoundland hostelries, for no matter how elegant the décor, the service is almost certain to be a little distraught and out of focus.

For inadequacies of service there are, however, compensations of a kind seldom found elsewhere. In St. John's we stayed in a motel which was quite literally being built around us — carpenters working round the clock in an attempt to get the place into some kind of order for the official opening in three days' time. After our first meal the cook emerged from her kitchen to apologize for the racket. Also to inquire about our welfare, origin, and intentions; discuss family life at length (with authority, for she was the mother of eleven); and advise us on sights to be observed in St. John's. Her uninhibited friendliness did not justify the execrable meals she cooked us but at least it made them easier to swallow.

'They shouldn't have done it,' a St. John's garage attendant said to us in a rich Irish brogue. 'I tell you they shouldn't have done it.'

'You mean the Highway? They shouldn't have built it?' my wife said. Alarmed, for already she was taking a proprietary interest in the Highway and didn't like hearing it slighted.

'It's not that,' the garage attendant said. 'It's not that at all. The Highway is a wonderful thing. But it's not ready. It won't be ready for years. I tell you they shouldn't have done it.'

He was one more of the many Newfoundlanders we talked with who are increasingly embarrassed by the arrival of dusty, ill-tempered travellers in dusty, battered cars — some from places as remote as Saskatchewan — who have been persuaded that the Trans-Canada Highway is a flawless stretch of hard-top reaching from Victoria to St. John's. Most of the people we talked with condemned the federal government for what they considered misleading or, at best, equivocal press releases regarding the true condition of the road.

'Sure we want tourists,' our garage attendant said. 'Some day. But not yet.'

At fairly regular intervals along the Highway we saw a sign bearing the slogan, 'We'll finish the drive in '65, Port aux Basques to St. John's, thanks to Lester B. Pearson.' But no one seemed to take the sign seriously except a few staunch St. John's Conservatives who regarded it as part of a Liberal plot to keep the government in power.

Our first night on the Highway we spent in Terra Nova Park 170 miles north-west of St. John's. Terra Nova is one of the newest of our national parks, still rather unlicked and raw. Accommodation for campers is adequate, for run-of-the-mill tourists, limited. The headquarters area of the park borders Newman Sound, an arm of the sea thrusting inland from Bonavista Bay. The sea-arm looks like a typical northern Canadian lake since it is almost completely surrounded by low hills studded with evergreen forest. At present travel through the park is restricted by lack of roads and trails, but visitors who take a boat out to sea may be rewarded — so we are told — by the sight of icebergs drifting in the chill Labrador current.

Forty-five miles west of Terra Nova Park the Highway by-passes Gander, the great transatlantic airport and surely the Siberia of air-force personnel. We remembered the lonely American wife bound for Argentia and thought how lucky she was. Gander sits in the middle of an evergreen desert, a dismal forest waste where even the lakes look disconsolate and sad. But the town of Gander itself is a wonderful and authentic piece of Americana — a suburbia without a city. Neat, well-painted houses radiate in crescents from a neat, well-painted shopping centre, and the housewives you see tripping along the crescents are neat and well-painted too and do more than their share, God bless them, to relieve the drabness of the world they inhabit, for they are mostly young and pretty and animated by hope of escape.

From Gander to Corner Brook, a distance of 234 miles, the Highway passes through what appears to be all but uninhabited country. There are one or two fair-sized towns — Grand Falls, Deer Lake — lying along the route, and occasionally a long arm of the sea reaches down from the north to break the monotony of the evergreen jungle, but most of the time the sea and the dwelling-places of men seem far away and you are aware of nothing except the vast, empty heartland lying south of the Highway. Elsewhere in Canada, Highway travellers are frequently oppressed by what Patrick Anderson has

called 'the pressure on the skull' of northern forest, rock, and muskeg; but in Newfoundland the pressure is from below. The forest is
overwhelming and all-pervading – in Marvell's phrase, 'annihilating
all that's made to a green thought in a green shade' – an obsessive
claustrophobic nightmare made endurable by occasional high ridges
which provide breathing-space and a broad view of dense forest, distant blue hills, and – particularly between Wolf Cove and Corner
Brook – spectacular mesa-like upthrusts of Appalachian rock.

Most visitors to Newfoundland are struck by the lack of any significant agricultural development, and annoyed by the consequent
difficulty of obtaining the fresh vegetables, fruit, and milk which on
the mainland are staples of everyday diet. Certain areas of interior
Newfoundland could undoubtedly be cultivated – if only for gardens
– with profit; but Newfoundlanders seem strangely reluctant to take
up the rake and hoe, or indeed to indulge in agricultural pursuits of

The Humber River

any kind. There is a traditional explanation of this reluctance. It is said that the early coast settlers did in fact attempt the raising of livestock, and imported several herds of mountain-goats on the assumption that the goats would be ideally suited to the terrain. When the last goat had fallen into the sea the Newfoundlanders abandoned all pastoral and agricultural pretensions and have lived on fish ever since.

At present the interior of the island is the domain of the great pulp-and-paper companies – Bowater (the biggest in the world) and Anglo-Newfoundland. The company towns – Deer Lake, Grand Falls, Corner Brook – are neat, well-ordered, and deadly dull. Grand Falls is buried in a green wilderness, but Corner Brook is superbly located on a wide bay and enjoys one of the finest natural settings of sea, hill, and forest in all Newfoundland.

Deer Lake and Grand Falls are for Newfoundland dull and conventional names almost certainly imposed on the towns by aliens. Newfoundland place-names, the spontaneous inventions of the early explorers and settlers, are almost always vivid, original, and apt. They would have delighted Henry David Thoreau who relished names suggesting that 'some simple and perchance heroic life might have transpired there'. Heart's Ease and Harbour Grace and Heart's Content and Maiden Arm and Lance Amour are names which owe nothing to tradition; they spring naturally from strong emotional reactions to environment. Taken together they are as melodious as a Shakespearean flower calendar – the creations of men who knew not Shakespeare but spoke his language.

But Newfoundland place-names do not always suggest bucolic bliss and sweet content. The darker passions, the disappointments, the stupidities, and the sins of mankind – as well as a certain grim humour on the part of their creators – are reflected in scores of names such as Famish Gut, Confusion Bay, Misery Point, God Almighty Cove, Barren Island (ironically set in Conception Bay), Gripe Point, Mistaken Bay, Witless Bay, Cuckold's Cove and Joe Batt's Arm. It is surely true that in no other part of earth are place-names so consistently suggestive of fundamental human emotion and experience – heroic and otherwise – as in Newfoundland.

The same simplicity, originality, and aptness characterize many of the words belonging to Newfoundland common speech – the speech of a people living in isolation for generations and therefore retaining and adding to the simple forthright vocabulary of the first settlers, not out of bookishness but experience and imagination. The genteel euphemisms of conventional, middle-class speech find no place in the native vocabulary. A word such as 'minny-ammer' sounds precisely like the object it names – an ill-tempered, whining child; and 'bangbelly', the Newfoundland word for a particularly indigestible kind of pancake, anticipates the explosive impact of the thing it stands for. And is there a lovelier or more suggestive word in any language than the Newfoundland 'merrybegot', meaning child born out of wedlock – a word rich in that warm humanity and understanding of man's frailty which our coldly legalistic 'illegitimate' denies?

Thirty miles north-east of Deer Lake, between Grand Falls and Corner Brook, lies the Sir Richard Squires Memorial Provincial Park, perhaps the most exciting of the many parks and picnic- and camp-sites being developed along the Highway in Newfoundland. The picnic area of the park we found hot and dusty and exposed, but a two minutes' stroll through the woods brought us to one of the most spectacular views in the interior of Newfoundland – the Salmon Falls of the Upper Humber River. A long stretch of the river

is visible from a look-out point several hundred feet above the falls, and the panoramic effect is stunning. While we were there we enjoyed the – to us – novel spectacle of salmon fighting their way upstream, bodies flashing silver in the sunlight as they strove to leap the seemingly insurmountable barrier of the falls. The river below the falls swarmed with fishermen in boats, canoes, hip-waders. We fell into talk with two of the fraternity who had given up for the day, a pair of jolly priests (one fat, the other lean) who had fished for salmon without success as far away as Labrador but were still optimistic and full of Christian faith. Today, they said, the fish weren't biting at all. While we chatted we saw a small boy hook a whopper from his boat. When he landed the salmon, with only a little help from his father, the two priests looked thoughtful but went away still (I am sure) full of faith.

We spent what we intended should be our last night in Newfoundland in a small, drab west-coast village a hundred miles 'down north' from Port aux Basques. The evening was cool and quiet and we walked for a long time along the splendid crescent-shaped beach of the bay. Except for a handful of children who observed us from a distance without much curiosity, we had the beach all to ourselves. The drive from Corner Brook in scorching heat over many miles of dust-ridden road-under-construction had been particularly nerve-wracking and exhausting, but the quiet of the evening and the smooth, hard-packed surface beneath our feet brought a degree of serenity to our agitated spirits, and restored tissue tone to our bruised flesh. Presently we saw a lone fisherman row in to shore with a catch of a dozen sea salmon. We talked to him for a while – with diffidence, for I am always a little ashamed to ask a man about his work out of what must appear to him idle curiosity. The fisherman was very young and he looked tired and cold. A poor catch, he said, which he would try to sell to the local stores.

Overhead, a plane from the multi-million American air base at Harmon Field a few miles north gleamed remote and alien in the light of the setting sun. The young fisherman did not look up at it.

For the last hundred miles in Newfoundland the Highway runs through heavy forest alternating with brief stretches of coastal beach and headland more barren and austere than those of the Avalon

Peninsula. As the road nears Port aux Basques the forest diminishes, gives way to rock and tundra, and straight ahead the Anguille Mountains thrust up boldly from sea level to a height of 2,000 feet. They are harsh, uncompromising hills to which a man might lift up his eyes but in no expectation of help.

When we reached Port aux Basques, a town huddled on and behind great naked rocks, we found that the ferry to the mainland, the *William Carson,* was already booked to overflowing. (In summer, reservations for the ferry should be made at least two weeks in advance.) We were lucky because had we been able to cross on schedule we would have missed our finest day in Newfoundland.

No one, it seems, pays much attention to the stretch of coast lying east of Port aux Basques – we couldn't find a description of it in any tourist brochure – and yet the thirty-mile run by car from Port aux Basques to Rose Blanche at the end of the road is one of the most novel and spectacular in all Newfoundland. The road, a new one, is surprisingly good and safe considering that much of it appears blasted out of solid rock. There are no trees at all along this stretch of coast – only rock and pond and peaty moss that gives under the feet like foam-rubber. The landscape reminded me a good deal of Connemara – wild, stony, and moorish, beautiful in a harsh, eerie kind of way. The hills are low and craggy and there is water on every level – rushing peat-coloured streams, waterfalls, big ponds, little ponds, insinuating sea-arms, superb seascapes – and at the end of the road the village of Rose Blanche.

Rose Blanche more than fulfils our dreams of what a Newfoundland village *ought* to look like. A long point of rock thrusts out into a deep bay and forms a natural harbour-pier. Houses perch on the point and the off-shore rocks and cling to the cliff-faces rising from the water's edge. The parts of the village are bound together by elevated wooden sidewalks snaking over water and rock and occasionally a substance that might pass for land. Since most places in the village are accessible by boat Rose Blanche suggests a Venice in miniature – if you can accept a fish-packing plant for a doge's palace and a rowboat for a gondola.

One house on stilts was provided with an ample supply of running

Fishermen's stages. Here the catch is unloaded and cleaned.

water by a stream which passed directly under it. We were much impressed by the terraced back-yard garden made of shored-up bits and pieces of earth and clinging to a sixty-degree rock-face. Flowers rioted alongside the rushing stream, and the potatoes in one corner of the garden were in bloom and doing well.

The names of the villages linked by the thirty-mile stretch of road remind us that Frenchmen, mostly from Jersey, were the first to fish and settle along the southern coast of Newfoundland. The Frenchmen have gone long since (nearly all the inhabitants of the coast are now Anglo-Saxon) but they have left a legacy of haunting names: Port aux Basques, Margaree, Isle aux Morts, Bay le Moine, Rose Blanche — echoes of an age long past and full of beauty and wonder. Who or what was the white rose? A flower? A ship? A woman? Who perished on the Island of the Dead and when and how? None of the natives could tell me, and I like to think that in that time long past hot-blooded Frenchmen killed one another for the love of a rose-white lady. Perhaps the captain's wife. The south coast of New-foundland is not a world to stimulate passion, and it is pleasant to fancy that at least once high romance had touched these bleak and lonely shores.

But the many humble memorials in the village churches to the drowned men 'whose hands shall toil the sea no more' (in the words of one such memorial) tell a grimmer, more realistic story.

Until the Highway is completed the tourist who has only a day or two to spend in Newfoundland would be infinitely better off explor-ing the really extraordinary beauty of the Port aux Basques–Rose Blanche country than pounding madly up the coast and through part of the interior to Corner Brook and back. (This is at present the popular two-day run.) Port aux Basques, being a harbour town and railway terminus, provides better-than-average accommodation and the villages provide all the rest.

The fishing, so we are told, is excellent.

One thing is sure. If the artists (Peggy's Cove variety) ever dis-cover Rose Blanche a new industry will be born in the village. And what the villagers will think of the artists is a subject of pleasurable speculation.

On board the *William Carson* we talked to a frail, elderly American couple, schoolteachers both, who had just completed the run to St. John's and back. White dust lurked in the folds of their clothes, and like ourselves they were still quivering from the effects of the wash-board.

'Why did you do it?' I asked.

'There's not much time left,' the woman said. 'I want to see as much as I can.'

She explained that until four or five years ago a heart condition had prevented her from doing much travelling; now she and her husband were seeking to satisfy that hunger for far-off places which the philosophers assure us is symptomatic of spiritual malnutrition. But it is, I think, logical that the elderly should travel much, for travel appears to suspend time; paradoxically, by moving about we persuade ourselves that we can command the sun to stand still, postpone its setting . . .

'But why Newfoundland?' I said.

The man smiled and looked embarrassed. 'The pioneer spirit, I guess,' he said. 'We wanted to see a place that hadn't been spoiled . . . before it's too late . . . . '

James Boswell would have understood the American schoolteachers perfectly. When Boswell visited the remoter islands of the Hebrides with Dr. Samuel Johnson he did so in the hope that 'we might there contemplate a system of life almost totally different from what we had been accustomed to see,' and 'find simplicity and wildness, and all the circumstances of remote time and place.'

Boswell would have understood the schoolteachers and he would have appreciated Newfoundland. The society we glimpsed there is one which is rapidly and inevitably disintegrating, unable to withstand the forces of progress represented by changed political status, increasing industrialization, social aid, and, when completed, the Trans-Canada Highway; but at present the old pattern is still to be observed in the areas lying outside St. John's and the company towns.

There is, and was, more in that society to deplore than to praise: the enormous gulf between rich and poor (which social aid and the federal Income Tax Department have done something to lessen), the expensive and inefficient system of denominational education (modified for the better in recent years but still sadly in need of drastic reform), neglect of the arts, and an outlook on life bounded for far too many by the limits of the local parish.

What is distinctive about Newfoundland society, what makes it 'a system of life almost totally different from what we have been accustomed to see' is a homogeneity found nowhere else in Canada (not even rural Quebec) and hardly elsewhere in the North American continent: a homogeneity that we associate with a much earlier time than the present – the consequence of people of the same blood living in comparative isolation and on a bare subsistence level for centuries. Of necessity the out-harbour Newfoundlanders have evolved their own mores, created their own culture, made and sung their own songs, and added to the language according to their need.

And on the physical level they have adapted their way of life to a harsh and treacherous and magnificent environment and in so doing have composed between themselves and that environment the harmony so finely expressed in the words of Newfoundland's — and Canada's — greatest poet, E. J. Pratt:

> Tide and wind and crag,
> Sea-weed and sea-shell
> And broken rudder—
> And the story is told
> Of human veins and pulses,
> Of eternal pathways of fire,
> Of dreams that survive the night,
> Of doors held ajar in storms.

The Heart Is Highland

NOVA SCOTIA

The old man – white-bearded, bottle-nosed, rheumy-eyed – sat on a bench on the pier at North Sydney. I think he was waiting for us.

'Applejohn the name is,' he said. 'Gamaliel Applejohn. *Cap'n* Gamaliel Applejohn.'

He jerked his head in the direction of the ocean. 'Boy an' man I've followed her nigh on seventy year. Fog-bound in a dory off the Grand Banks for a week in '91 . . . froze in the ice with old Bob Bartlett the winter of '06 . . . drug two thousand mile by a U-boat we harpooned in '15. Landed her in the end, but o' course the Navy claimed the credit . . . . '

Captain Applejohn cleared his throat and spat. 'You folks like to hear me sing "The Squid-Jiggin' Ground"? There's them will tell you she come from Newfoundland, that song did. But they're wrong. Dead wrong. Made her up myself . . . nigh on sixty year ago . . . .'

Captain Applejohn is the man I never met. In Nova Scotia or anywhere else. Various sources of information – in particular, one publicly owned – had led me to believe that our journey across Canada would be a succession of jolly and informative encounters with folksy characters sitting on benches (logs, stones, etc.) who shared the Ancient Mariner's passion for telling a good story. I had confidently expected to meet in the Maritimes tarry old yarn-spinning salts exuding local colour and rum fumes, hear Gaelic-speaking Cape Breton Scots assure me with tears in their eyes that still the blood iss strong the heart iss Highland ass we in dreams behold the Hebrides. And the West, I knew, was overrun by leather-skinned, crinkly-eyed farmers ready at the click of a tape-recorder to sum up in a succinct phrase (punctuated by a stream of tobacco-juice) the essential spirit of the prairies – 'She's a next-year country, son. Say, let's gather up a bucket of them goddam hailstones and make a freezer of ice-cream.'

I never met any of them.

I hesitate to suggest that these splendid folksy characters I had looked forward to meeting do not exist. Perhaps they were all off making tapes for the CBC.

Every trans-Canada traveller with an interest in his country's past should leave the Highway at North Sydney, as we did, and drive the forty-odd miles of excellent road (Nos. 5 and 22) to the once-great fortress of Louisbourg – now a National Historic Park – on the east coast of Cape Breton Island.

The fortress, built by the French shortly after the signing of the Treaty of Utrecht in 1713, was meant to command the Cabot Strait and safeguard the St. Lawrence waterway leading to Quebec and Montreal. When in 1744 war again broke out between France and Great Britain, a wild-eyed, comic-opera rabble of New England militia under the command of a Boston merchant, William Pepperell, laid siege to the undermanned fortress and captured it in just seven weeks. The siege involved much hard work hauling big guns into position over the muskeg swamps behind the fortress, but little loss of life.

What followed the light-hearted capture of the fortress was stark tragedy. The New Englanders found themselves obliged to garrison their prize during the following winter, and a succession of 'putrid fevers and dyssentrys' swept the camp. The young New Englanders had laughed at the French bullets; a man had a chance in a fair fight, and death in battle – *pro patria mori* – was a clean and honourable death. But dysentery and typhoid were something else again – they tore a man's entrails apart, gave him no chance to fight back. Before the winter was out nearly 1,000 of the frolicsome lads who had sailed with Pepperell lay in shallow graves on the windswept beach.

In 1748 – crowning insult to the pride of the living and memory of the dead – the fortress was given back to France.

Ten years later when the final battle for America was taking shape, Louisbourg was once more invested by a besieging army – no brave rabble of militia this time but 12,000 British regulars under the command of the veteran general Amherst and supported by a fleet of thirty-nine sail. Among Amherst's officers was a brilliant, neurotic brigadier named James Wolfe. The death in battle which Wolfe seems to have coveted so ardently almost claimed him on the beach of Gabarus Bay a few miles south-west of Louisbourg, but he lived to fight another day on the Plains of Abraham.

The French, hopelessly outnumbered and cut off from all sources of reinforcement and supply, fought with astonishing determination and gallantry. Hundreds of Englishmen died on the beaches, hundreds more in the dismal swamps behind the fortress; but in the long run God sided with the big battalions. After a five months' resistance Louisbourg surrendered, and for the last time the lilies of France fluttered down the flagstaff. The English under the direction of Admiral Foulweather Jack Byron, grandfather of the poet, razed the fortress with the utmost thoroughness, left hardly one stone of the Gibraltar of America standing on another.

And now the men of the National Parks Board are trying to put all the stones back again.

Perhaps what one needs to appreciate Louisbourg is not so much a sense of history as of elegy. Here and there an isolated headstone thrusts itself up from the lonely, haunted beach, honouring some segment of the thousands of nameless dead – puppets of those in the seats of the mighty – whose bones lie in the shallow earth; and the seagulls scream an enduring requiem. Shelley would have understood Louisbourg, for like the ruined statue of Ozymandias, half-buried in the desert sands, the fortress is a symbol of man's pride and folly and mortality. 'Nothing beside remains' – except a few piles of tumbled stones out of which curious men now seek to re-create the storied past.

We returned from Louisbourg to North Sydney in chastened melancholy mood, and from that dismal town, with a good Scots friend to guide us, drove west along the Highway towards the heart of Cape Breton. A mile or two out of North Sydney we cleared the dark, shabby houses and the swarms of children playing along the

34

Highway and drove through pleasant pastoral countryside which suddenly assumed new contours, fell away unexpectedly in deep valleys, rose in long, wooded ridges. Through a heavy haze we saw in the distance the dim outlines of hump-backed hills and knew we were approaching the Cape Breton Highlands.

The Highway crosses into the Highlands from Boularderie Island over one of the most beautiful bridges in Canada, a slender green filament suspended between water and sky. A long arm of the sea thrusts in here between great hills – like a Scandinavian fjord in miniature – to become part of the Bras d'Or Lakes system. When we crossed the bridge the sea-arm lay beneath us blue and unruffled, beautiful as a dream. On either side of the arm the hills rise up abruptly from the water's edge, and hills and water and sky combine to form a flawlessly balanced pastoral.

35

Cap Rouge in Nova Scotia

It has become a commonplace to suggest strong similarities between the Cape Breton and Scottish Highlands. The comparison is a purely sentimental one; for beyond the fact that both regions are overrun by Scots no similarities exist. The Cape Breton Highlands are soft, comfortably rounded, heavily wooded to the top; the Scottish Highlands are stark, jagged, aloof. A stranger to Cape Breton is immediately at home among the hills; in the Highlands of Scotland he for a long time feels himself an interloper, an alien.

We left the Highway about twenty miles out of North Sydney, drove north a short distance along a good gravelled road to Englishtown, and looked at the grave of Angus MacAskill, the Cape Breton giant who died in 1863 at the age of thirty-eight. MacAskill was seven feet nine inches tall and, so his epitaph informs us, 'a dutiful son, a loving brother, a true friend, a loyal subject, a humble Christian'. Nothing we know of the giant's life contradicts this lapidary tribute. Angus MacAskill was a gentle man who made a modest fortune, which he shared generously with relatives and friends, by exhibiting himself before the crowned heads of Europe and elsewhere. Queen Victoria reported herself much impressed, particularly when, so the story goes, MacAskill trod heavily on her best carpet, and cut out pieces – cookie-cutter fashion – with his heels.

The giant was even more celebrated for strength than for size, and it was while he was doing casual weight-lifting exercises with an anchor variously reported as weighing from one to one and a half tons that he received an injury which led to his early death.

Of the many accounts of MacAskill's life the most interesting – for a variety of reasons – is *The Cape Breton Giant: a Truthful Memoir*, written by a schoolmaster named James Gillis. The author, listing his credentials in a brief foreword, informs his readers that 'I was twice to the United States; I do not say so for the sake of boast,' and adds that 'this biography is the very best of the kind that was ever published . . . a superb representative of MacAskill's greatness . . . pleasurable, recreative, very instructive, and practically beneficial.' In the course of the memoir Gillis tells us that Robert Burns, whose birthplace MacAskill had visited during a tour of Scotland, 'lived a good life, a life of current sobriety, a life of superfluous honesty, and died happily, attended by his wife, bonnie Jean, and by his lovely friend, Jessie Lewyars'.

Every visitor to Nova Scotia should travel the full length of the Cabot Trail. The Trail can easily be reached from several points along the Trans-Canada Highway (St. Ann's is a logical turning-off point) and covered in a day over the fine paved road that circles three sides of the Cape Breton Highlands National Park and provides magnificent vistas at every turn. So I am told and believe, although we ourselves, driving counter-clockwise around the Trail, got no farther than Ingonish before the mist closed down completely. From the top of Cape Smoky, usually the most advantageous look-out point on the Trail, we saw nothing at all, but the drive up was worth while in terms of sheer physical sensation, for the road rises 1,200 feet in a little over a mile.

We drove back from Ingonish through the mist to St. Ann's, a charming village on a splendid, wide bay, where in summer the only Gaelic college on the continent opens its doors to students from half a dozen countries. Here men who 'have the Gaelic' give instruction in that ancient tongue, while other devoted upholders of old arts and ways teach handicrafts, Highland dancing, and, inevitably, the pipes. But for those of us who find the deliberate cultivation of the folk arts by a sophisticated society a little precious, St. Ann's is chiefly interesting as the one-time parish of that most redoubtable of Cape Breton preachers and personalities, the Reverend Norman McLeod.

Gold-medallist in moral philosophy at Aberdeen, a mighty man of God, and a prickly maverick, Norman McLeod sailed for Nova Scotia early in the nineteenth century with a boatload of evicted Sutherland crofters in his charge. He and his flock settled around Pictou in Nova Scotia, and were well established there when McLeod received a call from a Scottish settlement in far-off Ohio which he felt he could not ignore – particularly when the call was supported by an offer of good land to all members of McLeod's congregation who should accompany him. Under McLeod's supervision his parishioners built a ship (called 'the Ark' by such doubters as chose to remain in Pictou) and in 1820 minister and congregation set sail for Ohio, their intention being to reach that far-inland state via the Atlantic seaboard, the Gulf of Mexico, and the Mississippi River. But a providential storm blew the Ark into St. Ann's Bay. There – and no one who has seen the bay could blame them – the battered Argonauts resolved to stay.

For more than thirty years Norman McLeod ruled his flock at St. Ann's with justice not always tempered by mercy. There was in the man much of the quality and power of an ancient prophet of Israel and his God was unmistakably the God of the Old Testament. (Christ has always been a bit too gentle for the Norman McLeods of this world.) His parishioners idolized and feared and obeyed him; and when in his old age he again received a summons from an agent of the Almighty – in this instance his own son – to go forth in search of the promised land, they unquestioningly packed up their belongings and went with him.

The first of the ships carrying the Cape Breton Scots reached Australia, the land from which Donald McLeod had reported fair prospects, in 1852. But the Australian gold fever was then at its height and Norman McLeod, fearing that his flock might be contaminated by the precious bane, re-embarked and sailed another thousand miles to New Zealand.

There, near the northern tip of the North Island, he found his Eden. In Waipu several shiploads of Cape Breton Scots built up a flourishing community which still survives – as Scottish as anything to be found in Cape Breton and more so than anything in Scotland. And there in the year 1866 at the age of eighty-seven Norman McLeod died.

Cape Breton, it seems, has had more than its fair share of giants.

Perhaps the best known of all Cape Breton communities is the village of Baddeck, twenty miles along the Highway from St. Ann's in the heart of the lovely Bras d'Or Lakes country. (The term 'lakes' is a misnomer – the Bras d'Or waters are salt and form what is in reality a shallow inland sea.) Many celebrated persons have visited Baddeck and paid tribute to her charm and therapeutic powers, among them the American novelist Charles Dudley Warner, Mark Twain's collaborator in *The Gilded Age,* who spent a few weeks in the village in 1873 and recorded his impressions in *Baddeck and That Sort of Thing*: 'the most electric American, heir of all the nervous diseases of the ages, could not but find peace in this scene of tranquil beauty'.

The most famous of Baddeck's citizens was Alexander Graham

The lighthouse at Baddeck

Bell who built himself a summer home on Beinn Bhreagh (Beautiful Mountain). There he sponsored the first airplane flight in the British Empire and conducted a number of fascinating and extravagant experiments, including the breeding of multi-nippled sheep – no doubt with a view of producing lambs in litters. The museum on Beinn Bhreagh estate, displaying many of Bell's apparatuses – but no sheep – is open to the public. Bell, faithful to the end to his adopted community, is buried near by on the hill-top.

Our Scots friend had, she told us, been as far west as Calgary. 'Wonderful country,' I said. 'Don't you think so?'

She nodded. 'Very wonderful indeed. In Calgary everyone said to me, "Look at the mountains." And I'd raise my eyes and there they were. Beautiful and far off.

'Here in Cape Breton,' she added, 'I don't need to raise my eyes to look at the hills. They're beautiful – and all around me.'

And then she wished us God-speed with a Gaelic blessing we liked:

> *May your road rise with you;*
> *May the wind blow always at your back;*
> *May the good Lord hold you in the hollow of His hand.*

We crossed from Cape Breton Island to the Nova Scotia mainland over the deepest causeway in the world. Oddly enough, in binding Cape Breton closer physically to the rest of Canada the Canso Causeway appears to have intensified the determination of the Islanders to preserve their ancient ways unspotted from the world. The expression 'more Scottish than Scotland' really means something in Cape Breton Island. An annual gathering of the clans, a Gaelic college, a model lone shieling in the Cape Breton National Park, a proposed model village at Iona – these manifestations of fierce adherence to tradition lead one to suspect that in lonely houses on dark nights kilted Cape Breton clansmen gather to call down curses on the House of Hanover and drink toasts in purest usquebaugh to the King over the Water.

But who among these ardent champions of the old ways and days permitted the Gut of Canso to be renamed the Strait? This substituting of a dull, characterless word for a rich, full-flavoured one is the sort of thing that couldn't possibly happen in Newfoundland.

Nova Scotians complain with a good deal of bitterness that the Trans-Canada Highway passes through virtually none of the province's renowned beauty spots – Cape Breton is an obvious exception – and that the tourist who sticks faithfully to the Highway receives little impression of Nova Scotia's scenic variety. Certainly the true beauty of Nova Scotia, and the extent to which she is geared to the care and feeding of tourists, can only be appreciated by following the narrow, twisting, traffic-jammed coastal highways through Halifax and Lunenburg, around the Yarmouth tip where the beaches are wide and wind-swept and invested with a bleak grandeur hardly equalled elsewhere in Canada, and back up through Acadian villages, the lush Annapolis Valley – lovely in spring and autumn, dull in summer – and the country of Longfellow's Evangeline beside the roaring red waters of Fundy Bay. It must be admitted, though, that the delights which charm the eye even on such an extensive tour as this do not entirely justify the eulogy of one Horatio C. Crowell which we found printed on the backs of menus in several Nova Scotia restaurants and read between courses with great pleasure:

'Did it ever occur to you that the Creator may have left this little sea-girt peninsula until the last? . . . Did you ever think that when this world was coming out of chaos the Creator might have set aside ever so little of the congealing mass upon which to imprint His own special design? Have you not thought of the Divine Hand pressing a finger upon the soft clay, and behold, a valley here, another there? Have you not seen in the wonderful contours of hills and mountains of this land the Divine imagery of what hills and mountains ought to be? . . . Did it never seem strange to you that this is a land without tempest, or flood, or drought, or gale, or pestilence, and, if it did, did you ever think that the reason may be because it is God's land?'

'God's land.' Whatever reservations the outlander may feel, few Nova Scotians are likely to dispute Horatio Crowell's conclusion.

Admittedly, the Trans-Canada Highway doesn't do full justice to the beauties of Nova Scotia. But it must be remembered that the Highway is primarily a direct linking route between provinces and only incidentally a scenic driveway. After a magnificent beginning in

Cape Breton it follows an uninteresting but logical route from the Canso Causeway across the northern part of the province and through the narrow neck of the Chignecto Isthmus connecting Nova Scotia and New Brunswick. Antigonish, about thirty miles west of Canso, is a pleasant shabby town where the attractive, red-brick Georgian buildings of St. Francis Xavier University border the main street under great elm trees; but a mile or two beyond the town the forest closes in and there is little of interest to see until Truro is reached at the head of the Minas Basin.

Truro is an elm-shaded old town boasting an enormously efficient Tourist Information Bureau which offers the visitor every inducement – including free tickets to the Saturday-night harness races – to stay in town a few days and see the local sights and patronize local services. (The tourist industry is more highly developed in the Maritimes than anywhere else in Canada, and more highly in Nova Scotia than anywhere else in the Maritimes.) But sustained travel through heavy forest always induces in me a mortuary mood, and I was more interested in a Moslem cemetery on the outskirts of the town than in the horse races. The cemetery, a neat green plot beside the Highway, contains a dozen or so headstones bearing Arabic inscriptions, and two – conventional, incongruous – to the memory of men named Harris and inscribed with the far-from-Moslem sentiment, 'Sleep On, Beloved'.

No one I talked to could tell me anything about the cemetery; but the subsequent combined investigations (on my behalf) of the Truro Tourist Information Bureau, the Truro Board of Trade, and the Colchester County Historical Society destroyed any hopes I had of uncovering a dramatic tale of a far-eastern trader wrecked in the Minas Basin, or of mutiny and violent death striking down heathen crew and Christian officers. The prosaic explanation of the cemetery's existence is that the hundred-odd Moslem families of Nova Scotia have agreed upon Truro as the appropriate site of a central burying-ground. The headstones bearing English names and inscriptions are those of Moslems who for business reasons adopted Anglo-Saxon names at the time they were granted Canadian citizenship.

The Minas Basin, eastern arm of the Bay of Fundy, ends at Truro; and the tidal bore of the Salmon River which flows into the Basin on the outskirts of the town is a much advertised tourist attraction. Unfortunately our stay in Truro failed to coincide with a tidal in-rush at any civilized hour; and we can report only that when the tide is out the river is a mere trickle between red mud walls.

The traveller pressed for time can get a fine glimpse of rural Nova Scotia and the Minas Basin by taking a short run out of Truro through Old Barns and Clifton to Princeport on the Shubenacadie River. The Shubenacadie is a tidal stream channelled deep between red banks where the bore is said to put on a spectacular display. We made the run just at twilight, through pleasant farmlands dominated by huge dairy barns, consistently the largest we saw anywhere in Canada. It would be difficult to conceive of a more startling juxtaposition of landscapes – on one side of us a lush, conventional Arcadia, on the other the weird, mirage-like, red-mud flats of the Minas Basin running for miles into the light of the setting sun.

It is unfortunate that the Trans-Canada Highway could not have been routed via Highway No. 2 along the north shore of the Minas Basin to Parrsboro and thence straight north to Amherst. The additions in mileage and driving-time are insignificant (about twenty miles and half an hour) and the view over the Basin from No. 2 is one of the finest in Nova Scotia. The official Trans-Canada route over No. 4 is excellent for making time on, but hasn't much else to commend it. A few miles beyond Truro the forest takes over, and there is little to break the monotony of the next eighty miles except an occasional small lake, and the pleasant Wentworth Valley where the summer fishing and winter skiing are said to be excellent.

The Highway by-passes the desolate mining town of Springhill, scene of several appalling mining disasters – the last in 1958 – and still haunted by memories of the dead sealed underground. Beyond the town of Amherst it bursts out on to the Tantramar Marshes which after 200 miles or more of claustrophobic forest are a heavenly joy to a Westerner. The marshes are lonely, wind-swept, and teeming with life, both wild and domestic. Here as long ago as the seventeenth century French settlers cunningly diked the land and reclaimed it from the sea. The tidal rivers are now controlled by modern dams, but some of the old dikes are still to be seen, and the general aspect of the marshes has probably not changed greatly over more than three centuries. The radio masts of the Canadian Broadcasting Corporation overseas service tower over the hay-barns dotting the marshes; but the hay-barns, weather-beaten and unchanged in design for generations, appear the more enduring.

The last mile or two of highway leading to the Nova Scotia–New Brunswick border is fairly consistently a motel and restaurant strip.

The border exit – or entry if you are driving east – is much the most elaborate we saw in Canada. The Highway divides and flows around a lawn with a sunken flower-garden at its centre; an admirably staffed tourist bureau stands ready to serve tourists on their way in; and a gift shop waits to catch them on their way out.

When we were at the border things were relatively quiet, but we were told that at the height of the season a piper in full regalia is on hand to welcome the incoming tourist with a full-bellowsed rendition of 'Cock o' the North' or 'Scotland the Brave'.

So far no one appears to have thought of placing a piper on the exit side to play 'Will Ye No' Come Back Again'. Or perhaps Nova Scotians assume that anyone who has seen their province once will return without invitation.

This Other Eden

PRINCE EDWARD ISLAND

The road to the Island (No. 16) runs north-east for thirty miles from just inside the New Brunswick border to Cape Tormentine. We crossed by ferry from Cape Tormentine to Borden, a distance of nine miles, in dull cloudy weather, and my first impression of the island 'cradled on the waves' was unfavourable and not at all in agreement with that of Jacques Cartier who reported in 1534 that 'all this land is low and flat, the most delightful that may be seen and full of beautiful trees and plains. . . . It is of the best temperature one could desire and of great warmth. . . . In a word there was nothing lacking to the land but good harbours.'

(Cartier was the Island's first publicity agent, and local Chambers of Commerce draw on him heavily for appropriate quotations. They draw much less frequently on another distinguished European commentator, Richard Cobbett, who in 1830 described Prince Edward Island as a 'rascally heap of sand, rock and swamp . . . in the horrible Gulf of St. Lawrence' . . . a 'lump of worthlessness' bearing nothing but potatoes.) The farms, I thought, looked self-consciously well-groomed, as if waiting to have their photographs taken – not a crooked furrow or a ragged tree in sight, not a blade of grass out of place, nor a single pig wallowing in a mud-hole. And I was grievously offended by a sign I observed along the Highway a mile or two out of Borden – 'Hospitality is our Business'.

Hospitality, I explained to my wife, is a disinterested expression of innate kindness and generosity; and I reminded her of the story we had heard in Newfoundland of a visitor to an outport who, seeking accommodation in a private home, was assured that he could have bed and victuals but unfortunately no hospitality. The visitor en-

joyed a huge 'scoff' (supper), a comfortable chair before a roaring
fire, musical entertainment provided by the daughter of the family
('The Sweet By and By' and 'Who Threw the Overalls in Mrs.
Murphy's Chowder?' played on the family organ); but was made
increasingly confused by his host's frequent embarrassed references
to his inability to provide 'hospitality'. Until at last the host said,
'Now if you had come yesterday you could have had all you might
to lower down into 'ee, but someone told the Mounties on me and
this morning they come and took it all away.'

Newfoundlanders, I said, understood and gave concrete expression
to the true meaning of the word hospitality. They did *not* identify it
with a sordid commercial transaction.

'I bet we're going to be comfortable,' my wife said.

She was right as usual. At the end of our first day on the Island I
was prepared to concede that the Islanders *know* their business.
Hostelries are spotlessly clean, service a miracle of promptness and
efficiency, food unremarkable but well-cooked and no doubt full of
vitamins, and prices surprisingly modest. I confess I succumbed
without a struggle to the unromantic charms of efficiency, and con-
soled myself for my weakness with the recollection of the answer a
battered old veteran of two world wars had given me when I asked
him what attribute he considered most desirable in a commanding
officer. 'Competence,' he snapped. 'That's all — competence. I don't
give a damn if my commanding officer loves me like a mother and
tucks me in bed every night with a hot-water bottle — or if he hates
my guts. Just so long as every time he makes a move he knows exactly what he's doing and how to do it.'

The Islanders, I am sure, would delight my veteran friend. You
won't find out whether they love or hate you — indeed it is most
unlikely that they'll develop strong feelings about you one way or
the other and if they do they won't let them show — but they know
exactly what to do to make you comfortable and how to do it.

Hospitality *is* their business.

Efficiency, however, is not limited to looking after tourists. The
Islanders also know how to provide very well for themselves, even
under unusual and difficult circumstances. All of us are familiar with
tales of travellers marooned by violent natural upheavals — in farm-
houses, isolated inns, log cabins in the wilderness — and have been

pleasantly harrowed by accounts of subsequent sufferings occasioned by cold, hunger, overcrowding, hysteria, and sometimes childbirth. The Prince Edward Islanders, too, are sometimes trapped by floods and blizzards but they rarely allow such interruptions of the routine order of things to make them uncomfortable. A few years ago a sudden March blizzard forced more than forty highway travellers to take refuge in a wayside service station where they remained cut off from the rest of the world for three days. Their experience, however, left no scars. The service station was attached to a restaurant well stocked with the necessities of existence, including indoor plumbing; and those stranded included a bread-wagon driver with a load of fresh bread, a trucker with a load of cured meats, two professional cooks, and – to deal with colds, pregnancies, and the like – two nurses. No one familiar with the Islander character will dismiss such a happy conjunction of essential supplies and personnel as mere coincidence.

We travelled from west to east on the Prince Edward Island section of the Trans-Canada Highway, from Borden, the western point of landing, to Charlottetown, and thence to Wood Islands, the eastern terminus of the Highway. The Island terrain is gentle, undulating, and seemingly presents no obstacles to the road-builder. But appearances are deceptive. There is hardly any rock on the Island and much of the road-building material has had to be shipped in from the mainland at enormous cost. The absence of a solid rock foundation near the surface of the earth (on the Island itself and under the Northumberland Strait) is one of the factors weighing heavily against the construction of a nine-mile causeway across the Strait to the mainland. Apart from the complex engineering problems involved, the cost of such a causeway would probably be prohibitive, unless the proposal made a year or two ago by an imaginative Islander were adopted.

The proposal, placed before the public in the form of a letter to the press, urged that all organizations in Prince Edward Island, including service clubs, church groups, Boy Scouts, Girl Guides, the I.O.D.E., and the W.C.T.U., collaborate in a grand beer-and-whisky-bottle drive and dump the resultant collection of glassware into the Northumberland Strait. It was the correspondent's contention that if all the beer and whisky bottles emptied by the Islanders in a single year were thus disposed of, the nine-mile causeway would be complete.

Charlottetown, in contrast to the immaculately groomed countryside surrounding it, is a rather grubby, down-at-the-heels little city, unusually compact and hence a joy to the tourist in a hurry who can see everything mentioned in the brochures – Provincial Building, Confederation Room, Government House, Basilica, Prince of Wales College – in an hour or two if he wears sneakers and is in moderately good physical condition. The Provincial Building, where the provincial legislature meets with pomp and ceremony to debate issues usually dealt with by municipal councils, is the showpiece of Charlottetown. Built in 1852, it is stolidly classical outside – a refreshing change from the miniature St. Peter's typical of most North American legislative architecture – and surprisingly elegant within. The designers, instead of subscribing to the baroque excesses of their own time, returned at least part way to the elegant simplicity of the early nineteenth century. Unfortunately the rooms are too small to convey fully the effect of lightness and airy grace which the designers obviously aimed at; and the interior architecture of the Provincial Building, and particularly that of the famous Confederation Chamber where the Fathers of Confederation held their first meeting in 1864, can best be described as heavy-jowled Regency.

The provincial legislature is made up of two parties. In the view of at least one baffled observer the parties are indistinguishable from each other except that one is in, the other out.

Close to the Provincial Building the new Confederation Memorial Building, built with funds provided by the federal and provincial governments of Canada, was rapidly nearing completion. Dedicated to the fine arts, the Memorial Building is mighty in bulk, radical in design, and when completed will dominate the city's centre. No doubt it will be in itself an harmonious entity, but it seems legitimate to anticipate some incompatibility in proportion and design between the old and the new.

One of the most cherished possessions of the Anglican Church of St. Paul's in Charlottetown is the baptismal register recording the birth on August 24th, 1798, of Margaret Elizabeth Gordon, best known to posterity as the possible original of the fair Blumine of Thomas Carlyle's *Sartor Resartus*: 'We seem to gather that she was young, hazel-eyed, beautiful, and someone's cousin; high born and of high spirit; but unhappily dependent and insolvent; living, perhaps, on the not too gracious bounty of moneyed relatives.'

If this is indeed meant to be a description of Margaret Gordon, Carlyle permits himself some romancing. Margaret Gordon was of high spirit, dependent and insolvent, and no doubt beautiful. But hardly high born. Her grandfather on her mother's side was Governor of Prince Edward Island, but a man of no family; her father a penniless medical officer serving in a detachment of the Black Watch stationed in Charlottetown. Following Gordon's early death little Margaret was sent to Scotland to be reared by an aunt in Kirkcaldy. To Kirkcaldy in 1816 came a gangling unlicked cub of a schoolmaster named Carlyle, who promptly fell in love with beautiful high-spirited Margaret Gordon. But the dour aunt who was the girl's guardian had had enough of poverty – her brother's and her own – and looked with disfavour on the young schoolmaster, a man of no worldly prospects. Besides, there already existed an understanding of sorts between Margaret Gordon and another suitor.

Margaret Gordon's last letter to Carlyle, written immediately before her removal from Kirkcaldy to London, makes clear her awareness of a power in the man far beyond that of common mortals, and of a growing arrogance which must already have made him an uncomfortable companion: 'Genius will render you great. May virtue render you beloved! Remove the awful distance between yourself and ordinary men by kind and gentle manners . . . I give you not my address, because I dare not promise to see you.'

There is not much evidence to support the romantic notion that Margaret Gordon loved young Thomas Carlyle; but even had she done so we can hardly regret her escape from the fate that befell Jane Welsh. Margaret Gordon married Alexander Bannerman, a merchant of substance, and in 1851, half a century after leaving Prince Edward Island, returned to the town of her birth as Governor's lady. Lady Bannerman was esteemed throughout the Island for her intellect, good works, and amiable demeanour; but such is our appreciation of intellect, good works, and amiability that no doubt she would have been forgotten long since had not a great man loved her.

The Highway from Charlottetown to Wood Islands passes through characteristically pleasant, unexciting countryside, less sleekly groomed than that between Borden and Charlottetown but richer in historic interest. At Belfast, twenty-five miles out of Charlottetown and a mile north of the Highway (the turn-off is at the village of Eldon), stands the lofty-spired Presbyterian Church of St. John's, built in 1823 by Highland settlers brought out twenty years earlier by that most assiduous and visionary of colonizers, the Earl of Selkirk. To most of us the name Selkirk Settlement means the Red River Colony, but the Belfast colony on Prince Edward Island preceded that of Red River by nine years. No doubt it has been largely overlooked because its progress was peaceful to the point of dullness, unimpeded by bitter conflict and bloody massacre. The 800 Highland Scots, most of them from the Isle of Skye, who formed the settlement, cleared the land in remarkably quick time, built modest homes, lived the prosaic lives of typical bush pioneers, and in the end created one of the most productive farming communities in Prince Edward Island.

St. John's Church, built by community labour, is a handsome structure – spire modelled after a design by Wren – but the dour Calvinism of its builders and adherents is reflected in the framed verses of Scripture which we observed adorning the walls of the basement Sunday School room – 'the soul that sinneth it shall surely die . . . without the shedding of blood there can be no remission of sins . . . '

In the extensive graveyard surrounding the church we found a knowledgeable Old Mortality hard at work cleaning and restoring headstones. He talked of the dead of a hundred years ago as if they were his familiars, and showed us the grave of Mary Douglass, the Earl of Selkirk's putative daughter, who came to the colony when a little girl and died there at the age of sixty. Just outside the churchyard stands a memorial inscribed in Gaelic and English, 'In Memory of the Scottish immigrants who came to the Island by Lord Selkirk's ships the Polly, the Dykes and the Oughton, in August, 1803,

Beach at Cavendish

and made homes for themselves and their children in the woods at Belfast.'

A mile or two along the Highway beyond Eldon, another turn-off leads west to the recently established Selkirk Provincial Park, a charming picnic- and camp-ground overlooking Orwell Bay. The picnic area borders a gloomy little evergreen copse which was the graveyard of French settlers in the days before the expulsion of the Acadians. The graveyard serves to remind us that the Island was originally claimed for France, perhaps by Champlain, early in the seventeenth century and named Ile St. Jean, and that it was held more or less continuously by the French until the expulsion of the Acadians from the Maritimes in the 1750s. In 1798 the present name was adopted in honour of Prince Edward, son of George III, at that time an officer with the British forces in America. Edward is best known to history as the father of Queen Victoria.

Wood Islands, where it is possible to catch a ferry to Caribou, Nova Scotia, marks the eastern terminus of the Trans-Canada Highway in Prince Edward Island. From Wood Islands we explored northwards over excellent red-dirt roads through heavily wooded and unexpectedly unkempt countryside as far as Montague, a pleasant old town on a once-beautiful but now polluted river. From Montague we pushed on north-east to the Bay of Fortune where artists and writers from the United States are said to congregate in large numbers. We saw great stacks of lobster-pots on the dock but no artists or writers — perhaps because the mist had rolled in from the sea and reduced visibility to a few yards.

Green Gables

Although the Trans-Canada Highway runs for only seventy miles through Prince Edward Island it provides an excellent base route from which to strike off on convenient side-roads to many points of interest scattered throughout the Island. And almost everyone, I suspect, is sooner or later drawn, as we were, to Cavendish National Park – a stretch of splendid beach on the north shore twenty-five miles long and half a mile wide – and to Canada's most popular literary shrine, a house called Green Gables.

Lucy Maud Montgomery doesn't rate much space in our anthologies or histories of Canadian literature. But her shade (and her publisher) can afford to laugh at the anthologists and historians, who are themselves nearly all forgotten overnight, for her books continue after half a century to sell by the thousands. Lucy Maud Montgomery wrote *Anne of Green Gables* more than fifty years ago, and she herself has been dead for twenty, but Green Gables, a charming, old-fashioned green and white house on the outskirts of the charming, old-fashioned village of Cavendish, swarms from morning till night with visitors of all ages, shapes, and sizes, to each of whom the little red-headed, green-eyed Anne is a familiar, a friend. I have visited only one other shrine so crowded with devotees – the Brontë parsonage in Haworth. The gloom-ridden, spectre-haunted home of that tragic sisterhood is a far cry indeed from

Green Gables, where all is sunlight and good cheer, and a golfer playing the ninth hole of the Cavendish course is likely – if he should be heavy with his approach shot – to put his ball through the living-room window.

Let us not begrudge Lucy Maud Montgomery the uncritical adulation of thousands of youngsters and grown-ups. She was sentimental, she violated all the rules of plausibility, her knowledge of human nature was superficial, she had no philosophy, and, naïvely believing that God's in His heaven all's right with the world, no tragic view of life. But she possessed the power – beside which more sophisticated literary talents are as inconsequential vapours – to breathe life into the people of her imaginings; and in *Anne of Green Gables* she created a character who has become a part of North American folklore.

What particularly impressed me about Green Gables was the fact that the pilgrims who swarmed eagerly through the old house from basement to attic had come to see the home not of L. M. Montgomery but of Anne.

I am convinced that the man who finds the world too much with him should go into a retreat for a couple of weeks, or else to Prince Edward Island which is practically the same thing. For many days before reaching the Island my wife and I had been pounding over crowded highways encompassed by heat and noise and dust and confusion. Our bodies were tired, our nerves were frayed, and I personally hated the whole world, and in particular the fools who dawdled along the Highway at sixty miles an hour and held us up. But after a day or two on the Island we found ourselves chatting amiably at meal-times – even breakfast – in voices that were quiet and restrained; on the Highway we laughed contemptuously at the fools who rushed past us at forty miles an hour; and in the shops my wife accepted with the utmost equanimity that fact that all mercantile transactions were conducted – so she assured me – in slow motion and triplicate. The improvement in our dispositions was matched by that in our bodies. All aches and pains fled away and our pulses slowed down remarkably but never quite stopped.

When Marshal Grouchy, the man blamed by some historians for

losing the battle of Waterloo because he couldn't find the Prussian Army, was living in exile in Prince Edward Island he did *not* write his memoirs. He waited till he got back to France. It seems inconceivable that a military man (retired) should miss the opportunity; but the truth is that the arts do not flourish in the Garden of the Gulf. Art thrives on social conflict, economic instability, emotional turmoil, and sin – all the elements which make for strife and heroic resolution. There is no social conflict in Prince Edward Island – even the French and the English get along very well with each other; generous federal subsidies help to sustain a stable economy; and the Islanders seem indisposed to consume any forbidden fruit except home brew. They are a contented people; and because they are content they read but they don't write. (L. M. Montgomery is a notable exception.) They look at pictures but they don't paint. No doubt they sing and listen to Don Messer but they don't compose. They feel no need to do any of these strenuous creative things because they have few powerful emotions to express. Life on the Island is pitched in a low key; it is placid, unspectacular, without great heights or depths – like the land which sustains it.

Prince Edward Island is snug, parochial, perhaps a little self-satisfied. To the Islanders, the world beyond their own shores doesn't matter much. They look in upon themselves and their possessions – their fine red soil and rich pastures and sleek dairy cows and well-stocked piggeries and abundant potato fields and fine trotting horses – and what they see is so good and satisfying that there is no need to look anywhere else. And if occasionally a man wants a little excitement there's almost sure to be a lobster festival going on somewhere (Don Messer and his Islanders supplying the music), and harness races to look forward to every Saturday night.

The tourist is likely to find the Garden of the Gulf immensely restful, but after a while a little dull – just as he would have found that other Garden before the Fall. But he leaves it with a sense of physical well-being, an assurance of value received for his money, and perhaps a heightened awareness of what Lord Dufferin meant when he said that Prince Edward Island became a part of the Dominion in 1873 under the impression that it was annexing the rest of Canada.

Loyalist Country

NEW BRUNSWICK

The Highway leads into New Brunswick through the Tantramar Marshes, past a tourist information bureau serving the interests of both New Brunswick and Prince Edward Island. Fort Beauséjour lies on the left-hand side of the Highway, the road to Cape Tormentine and Prince Edward Island on the right, the shabby old town of Sackville straight ahead.

Fort Beauséjour was built by the French in 1751 to guard the narrow neck of land – the Chignecto Isthmus – leading to French Canada. It fell, almost without a fight, to the British in 1755. The fort has recently been restored and a museum erected on the site; but Beauséjour is no Louisbourg, and the restoration fails to communicate much sense of time past. Perhaps the restoration has been a little too neat and housewifely; no ghost accustomed to fallen masonry and overgrown footpaths could walk in comfort over those immaculately curry-combed earthworks and manicured lawns. But Fort Beauséjour lies less than a mile off the Highway and is well worth a visit if only for the fine view it commands of the marshes and the Cumberland Basin.

Sackville, ten miles inside the border on the western approaches to the marshes, is a pleasant, unpretentious town lying humble at the feet of Mount Allison University. The Mount Allison campus is a lush meadow of greenery dotted with fountains and lily ponds and lined with stately trees in the best groves-of-academe tradition, and one expects all professors who wander within its confines to wear gowns and long white beards and be absent-minded. Unfortunately the numerous and rather garish new university buildings are violently at odds in colour and design with the mellow red-brick halls of an older time, and the resulting discord seems unlikely to encourage habits of philosophic speculation.

Beyond Sackville the Highway plunges once more into heavy forest, re-emerging to provide the traveller with some splendid forest-and-river vistas from the heights above Moncton. Moncton is a bustling, self-confident town, the fastest-growing in the Maritimes, which boasts and exploits two celebrated natural phenomena – the Magnetic Hill and the tidal bore of the Petitcodiac River. My wife insisted that we test the alleged powers of the hill on the grounds that she *liked* doing stupid things, but she afterwards acknowledged that 'doing' the hill exceeded the permissible limits of stupidity. The hill provides the kind of optical illusion anyone who has ever travelled mountain highways is familiar with – your car appears to be travelling down-hill when it is really travelling up, and vice versa.

The attraction of the hill is such that several motels, the inevitable gift shop, and an inn boasting no fewer than five dining-rooms (which must be a record of some sort) flourish at its foot.

Tidal bores are extremely difficult to avoid in the vicinity of the Minas Basin or Chignecto Bay. The Petitcodiac bore is said to be at its best in spring and fall, during the out-of-tourist season. We missed it, because when we saw the river the tide was going out instead of coming in.

Forty miles west of Moncton we turned off the Highway and made a twenty-mile detour into Fundy National Park, a typically Maritimes preserve of forest land and sea-shore, bordering Fundy Bay. It was raining hard when we entered the Park, and the campers we saw emerging from their cocoons in the camp-site near the gates looked bleached and puckered as if they had been in water a long time.

Happily the rain stopped long enough to permit us to form some impression of our surroundings. The road leading to Park Headquarters climbs at one point to a height of 1,200 feet, and the marine views are impressive. Facilities are attractive and admirably supervised, but seemed to us inadequate to cope with the invading hordes of which we formed a part. We found it difficult to park, impossible to obtain a meal. But the views were fine even through the mist, and we were delighted to find a covered bridge leading out of the park and across the Alma River into Alma village, an agreeable huddle of houses under the shadow of a mighty headland.

Sussex, lying in a broad pastoral valley fifty miles west of Moncton, is one of the pleasantest towns in New Brunswick and a well-known handicrafts centre. I have always looked with suspicion on communities self-consciously dedicated to the cultivation of the folk-arts. Handicrafts, like folk-singing, are too often assumed to be good and beautiful *per se* without regard for the intrinsic quality of the thing produced. But several at least of the Sussex craftsmen are highly trained sophisticated artists whose work is a joy to behold.

Two Netherlanders, Barth and Lucie Wttewaall, are silversmiths of wide and growing reputation who occupy a delightful tree-shaded studio standing just a little way back from the Sussex main street. The Wttewaalls make use not only of silver for their creations but also of native stones – carnelians, agates, greenstones – which they gather from near-by streams.

The Wttewaall story is an unusual one. The couple established themselves on a farm near Sussex shortly after the end of the Second World War, built greenhouses, and grew roses which had a wide sale throughout the Maritimes. In 1954 they took a basic two-weeks' course in metal-working offered by the New Brunswick Department of Handicrafts, and only a few months later won a major award at the Canadian National Exhibition for a silver necklace set with local greenstones. Their success as silversmiths, achieved at a time of life when few of us are looking for new fields to conquer, has been such that they have been able to give up their greenhouses and devote all their time to the new craft. This is the kind of success that should be an immense encouragement to those who take handicrafts courses and an even greater encouragement to those who offer them.

Here too in a lovely old white house on a hill-side overlooking the town lived those two extraordinarily gifted artists in pottery, Kjeld and Erica Deichmann. Kjeld Deichmann, a descendant of

Sören Kierkegaard and appropriately a graduate of the University of Copenhagen, settled with his bride on a farm on the Kennebecasis River near the city of Saint John. But the creative urge could not be satisfied by growing crops and raising livestock, and presently the Deichmanns, after studying pottery techniques in Denmark, entered upon a long period of painstaking and often frustrating experimentation with various kinds of clay available in the Maritimes. The period of apprenticeship and experiment culminated, about twenty-five years ago, in the production of stoneware and porcelain pieces of flawless workmanship and highly imaginative and original design. Kjeld Deichmann was the 'maker' in the partnership, the manipulator of the clay, Erica the designer and finisher. A few years ago the Deichmanns left Banklands, their farm home overlooking the Kennebecasis, and removed to Sussex; and there in 1963 their partnership was ended by Kjeld's all-too-early death. But long before the time of his dying he and Erica had been internationally recognized as Canada's finest potters. It is given to few men to leave behind so many exquisite memorials of their being.

The Highway drive from Sussex to Fredericton, about seventy miles, is a delight all the way. There is dense forest, to be sure, but its pressure is eased at frequent intervals by the sight of picturesque villages, slow-flowing rivers, and hills which rise several hundred feet above the surrounding terrain, and by occasional tantalizing glimpses of the blue and silver waters of Grand Lake. And after crossing the Jemseg River the Highway begins an uninterrupted run of more than 200 miles alongside that loveliest of Maritime rivers, the St. John.

The country between Jemseg and Fredericton, and indeed for many miles up-stream above Fredericton, is deep-meadowed, happy, fair. Cows graze knee-deep in lush pasture grass, elm trees line the Highway on either side and sometimes meet to form an arch overhead, flower-bordered white frame houses bask in the warm sunlight, and the broad island-studded river flows slowly past on its way to the sea. All the elements of the idealized rural scene are here — the kind of scene I saw on farm-machine-company calendars when I was a small boy on the homestead, which even then seemed to me too beautiful to be true. But rural New Brunswick at its best makes any calendar picture of rustic pulchritude I ever saw look a little bit drab.

My wife and I saw with understandable emotion the spires of Fredericton thrusting their tips above the elms which are the chief glory of the city. A long time ago Fredericton had been our home for five years, and we remembered vividly our first day in the city and all the things we saw and did. We remembered the long quiet reaches of the river we had walked beside to soothe our fearful spirits – for I had assumed a new job in what was for both of us an alien world; remembered the main street sleeping peacefully in the sun, and the aged man shuffling along the sidewalk, clutching a brown-paper parcel to his chest and mumbling to an equally aged companion, 'Every time I get married I buy a new pair of shoes.' Remembered above all the unostentatious hospitality of those who could have felt no responsibility for us beyond that of one human being for another. We were apprehensive because we knew that things would not be the same, and we braced ourselves to face the changes that a quarter of a century brings to people and places.

We were right to do so, for things were not the same. The town's once-quiet main street was now a clotted, inadequate, one-way traffic artery; the University of New Brunswick, twenty-five years ago a modest clutch of antique buildings in the middle of a hayfield, now sprawled in a pleasing red-brick-Georgian harmony over half a square mile of immaculately groomed hill-side; and many a quiet country lane where we had delighted to walk long ago was now overrun by the cottages of suburbia. Above all, we ourselves were not the same. The resilience of youth had gone from us, and we were no longer ambitious, for we knew what we could and could not do.

But some things were the same. The trees which spread their branches across the streets in arches a hundred feet above the ground so that everywhere you walk in sun-dappled shade; the grey old cathedral, replica of an Old Country church in a town bearing the unlikely name of Snettisham, but over the generations acquiring a patina and personality uniquely its own; the houses built at the height of the late Victorian horrors, bedizened on the outside with gingerbread fretwork, porticos, turrets, catwalks, but inside magnificently spacious – fit residences for the prosperous merchants and lumber princes and gaggles of servants who lived in them during those ample days before the turn of the century. Even today a surprising number of Frederictonians, many of them far from prosperous, are prepared to forgo the physical conveniences of a packaged suburbia for the kind of gracious living which is the

concomitant of space – high ceilings, broad curving staircases, and fortified back gardens. It is significant that few apartment houses have been built in Fredericton – even though the town has doubled its population since the Second World War – and virtually none in the wonderful, tree-shaded, older residential areas along the river and up the valley slopes.

Something else we found unchanged by the passage of the years – a hospitality which is neither a business nor a duty but an expression of simple unaffected human kindness and regard for one's fellow man.

The history of Fredericton is uneventful. Originally a trading-post and military camp called St. Ann's Point, it grew into a market town to meet the needs of disbanded officers and men who had taken up land in the vicinity. In 1785 Thomas Carleton, the first Governor of New Brunswick, decreed that St. Ann's should be the capital of the province, and that it should henceforth be called Fredericks Town 'after his Royal Highness the Bishop of Osnaburg' – otherwise Frederick Augustus, second son of George III, a titular bishop and incompetent general.

The half-pay officers of the disbanded regiments were joined by large numbers of Empire Loyalists from the United States. The Loyalists prospered in lumber in the days of the great sailing ships; they built the cathedral and the university and they planted the elm trees. No one who grew up in the gracious houses under the elms ever wanted to leave, so that family tradition has played a strong part in creating the unique atmosphere of the town, an atmosphere compounded of an innate conservatism, a love of fine but not necessarily expensive things, and a life-pace which gives one time to stand and stare and enjoy.

In a local cemetery there stands a headstone to the memory of a man who at the age of ninety-two 'turned to God and thereafter lived a good life'. In his refusal to be hurried he was a true Frederictonian.

In the years immediately following the Second World War something happened which threatened to alter drastically the Fredericton way of life and charge that dreamy town against its will with an alien and disturbing vitality. A New Brunswick native son, the dynamic, block-busting, enormously wealthy Lord Beaverbrook adopted Fredericton as one of his principal beneficiaries, and with characteristic enthusiasm and disregard of all possible objections to his plans proceeded to tip his bottomless cornucopia over both town and university.

Evidences of His Lordship's beneficence and impact come into view as you enter Queen Street from the east. On the left-hand side stands a Beaverbrook-donated civic auditorium; on the right the Beaverbrook Art Gallery, the Lord Beaverbrook Hotel, and in a park adjoining the hotel a massive statue of Lord Beaverbrook. (Few mortals, however eminent, have been privileged to see their own memorials, but Lord Beaverbrook was always a man in a hurry.) At His Lordship's feet a mamma beaver and baby beaver squirt water into a pond twenty-four hours a day.

The paintings in the Beaverbrook Art Gallery, a beautifully proportioned building commanding through an arched central window a superb view of the river, are almost exclusively British and Canadian as befits the collection of a staunch Empire man; but a few foreigners, including Salvador Dali, have been allowed to creep in. Gainsborough, Reynolds, Constable, and Turner are among the traditional British masters represented, Graham Sutherland and Stanley Spencer perhaps the most interesting of the moderns. The Canadians include Krieghoff (represented by over thirty canvases), Paul Kane, Horatio Walker, Homer Watson, Clarence Gagnon, Emily Carr, most of the Group of Seven, and a sprinkling of contemporaries, among them Pegi Nicol MacLeod, Paul-Emile Borduas, and New Brunswick's own Alexander Colville, Miller Brittain, and Jack Humphrey.

The *chef d'oeuvre* of the gallery in terms of size (13½ by 10 feet) is the Salvador Dali canvas 'Santiago El Grande', depicting the ascent of St. James on horseback into heaven. The saint is flanked by two Dali portraits, one of Lady James Dunn (now Lady Beaverbrook) in falconer's costume – also on horseback but not going anywhere – the other of Sir James Dunn in a toga.

Another grouping of more than usual interest consists of three Graham Sutherland portraits – Mrs. John David Eaton (full length), flanked by Somerset Maugham and Edward Sackville West (top halves only).

One painting which appealed to me strongly was a beautifully uncluttered prairie scene in yellows by that excellent Winnipeg artist, George Swinton. My appreciation was not shared by two other viewers, ancient ladies who, I suspect, had passed most of their lives under the spreading elms, and whose comments, delivered in the loud rasping tones of the almost deaf, were audible in the farthest reaches of the gallery.

'Not a thing in it,' the first lady said.

'Not a thing,' the second echoed. 'Not even a tree.'

Lord Beaverbrook's gifts to the university (of which he was inevitably Chancellor) in buildings, scholarships, and equipment are equally as munificent as those he bestowed on the town. His Lordship was, of course, a gentleman of imperious temper and commanding ways, and there is evidence to suggest that occasionally faculty patience may have been tried to the point where patience ends and testiness begins. Indeed, there was a time when it appeared that the chief function of the president of the university was to be neither academic nor administrative but priestly – that of intermediary between God and man.

Lord Beaverbrook was a generous if at times nerve-wracking friend to both town and gown, and Fredericton is grateful, but not obsequious; and it seems unlikely that any citizen of the town would approve the 'official' description of the recently concocted New Brunswick tartan 'highlighted by beaver brown to express appreciation of our most eminent benefactor'. In the long run the town will no doubt do with Lord Beaverbrook as it has done with all those, great and mean, who have fallen under its spell in the past – quietly absorb him. Fredericton is the kind of place that puts its stamp on people rather than the other way about.

A town as strongly endowed with individuality as Fredericton is inevitably the kind of place to breed and attract artists. Dedicated painters, including Pegi Nicol MacLeod and Lucy Jarvis, established a flourishing art school in conjunction with the university at a time when money was scarce and appropriate gallery space virtually non-existent; and they and their work have not been entirely forgotten

in these days of the new dispensation. Poets have found audiences in
Fredericton almost since the day of its founding. Jonathan Odell, a
'loyal' New Jersey clergyman at the time of the American Revolu-
tion, wrote savage satires against the rebellious colonists —

> Though faction by falsehood awhile may prevail
> And loyalty suffers a captive in jail,
> Britain is roused, rebellion is falling.
> God save the King!

— and eventually packed up his cassocks and chasubles and joined
the great Loyalist migration north. Odell played a prominent part in
the development of the city and the province. He was the first provincial secretary, and built himself the fine house which is now the
deanery of Christ Church Cathedral. The Odell woods, twenty-odd
years ago a delightful country walk but now a part of suburbia, were
named after Jonathan Odell's son William who succeeded his father
as provincial secretary and lived the life of a country squire.

In a quiet corner of the University of New Brunswick campus
stands a memorial to that admirable posse of Fredericton poets — Sir
Charles G. D. Roberts, Bliss Carman, Francis Sherman — who a
generation or more ago galloped madly off in pursuit of Truth and
Beauty. Although they never quite caught up, they served their age
perhaps better than any succeeding group of poets in Canada has
done, and their achievements and memory are still cherished in a
town always friendly to poetry and ghosts. Today the poetic tradition
which began with Odell survives in the work of the University of
New Brunswick poets, including Alfred Bailey, Elizabeth Brewster,
and Fred Cogswell, much of whose verse has appeared in that excellent local literary journal, *The Fiddlehead*.

Nearly all things which possess in themselves no positive sexual attributes but which stir powerful emotions in the heart of man — a
ship, an automobile, a tornado, a river — we denominate feminine.
And of all Canadian rivers the St. John is surely the most feminine
— broad-bosomed, maternal, life-giving, a veritable madonna. Feminine too in her contradictions, in her power (familiar to all married
men) to reverse the course of her progress and flow backwards in
defiance of reason and natural law.

The Trans-Canada Highway follows the graceful curves of the St. John all the way from Fredericton to Edmundston, 175 miles upstream and only ten miles from the Quebec border. Unlike Nova Scotia, New Brunswick is admirably served by the Highway. No doubt the North Shore and Miramichi routes have their champions, but most visitors to the province are agreed, I think, that of all possible drives in New Brunswick the one up the St. John via the Trans-Canada Highway is the loveliest and most relaxing.

The country through which the Highway passes – for the most part pleasant, unexciting farmland interrupted from time to time by delightful old-world green and white villages – was settled very much after the pattern of Fredericton, and its history is a little lacking in

colour and drama. The St. John Valley was never the scene of man's slaughter, and the struggle to tame the land and cut down the forest has been routine.

Many of the communities above Fredericton (Woodstock is an obvious example) were, like Fredericton, originally settled by half-pay officers, disbanded soldiers, and United Empire Loyalists, and consequently share the capital city's leisurely attitude towards life, with no benevolent tycoons to prod them into occasional vigorous action. The ambitious have long since gone elsewhere – most of them, it seems, to the Far West to occupy academic posts never below the rank of dean – and those who remain are prepared to forgo the prizes to be won at great price in the market-place so that they may move through life at a pace which is out of step with the rest of the world. The New Brunswickers who live along the St. John seem to have absorbed something of the tranquillity of the river; they have learned that great elms (if spared the blight) and poetry and salmon-fishing and quiet river reaches are more conducive to peace of mind than back-yard swimming pools and Cadillacs. Not that they are hostile to swimming pools or Cadillacs—but first things first.

Between Fredericton and Woodstock two modest streams join the St. John — overgrown creeks, really — with no claim to notice except for the charm of their original names, a charm preserved in a genial lyric composed nearly one hundred years ago by a Dalhousie professor of English, James de Mille:

> Sweet maiden of Passamaquoddy,
> Shall we seek for communion of souls
> Where the deep Mississippi meanders,
> Or the distant Saskatchewan rolls?
> Ah no! in New Brunswick we'll find it —
> A sweetly sequestered nook —
> Where the sweet gliding Skoodawabskooksis
> Unites with the Skoodawabskook. . . .
>
> Let others sing loudly of Saco,
> Of Passadumkeag or Miscouche,
> Of the Kennebecasis or Quaco,
> Of Miramichi or Buctouche;
> Or boast of the Tobique or Mispec,
> The Mushquash or dark Memramcook;
> There's none like the Skoodawabskooksis
> Excepting the Skoodawabskook.

At Hartland the Highway crosses the river from west to east, and Hartland's most cherished exhibit, the world's longest covered bridge (1,282 feet), stands in full view. Covered bridges — and there are many of them in the Maritimes — are endowed with a quaint, old-world charm which no doubt justifies their preservation, although aesthetically they are no more pleasing than the elongated cow-sheds they greatly resemble.

The upper St. John was once one of Canada's great lumbering

domains, the home of Paul Bunyan before Michigan, Wisconsin, and Minnesota appropriated him, and celebrated in scores of fine ballads ranging in mood from the pathetic, as in the well-known 'Jam on Jerry's Rock'

> Six of the mangled bodies a-floating down did go,
> While crushed and bleeding near the bank was that of young
>   Munroe.

to the Homeric, as in 'The Scow on Cowden's Shore'

> There were men from many places, of many different races,
> With pale and swarthy faces, I cannot name them o'er,
> Island men and Restigouchers, Nashwaakers and Pugmooshers,
> All assembled here together round the Scow on Cowden's Shore.
>
> There's men from Oromocto, some more from Richibucto,
> From Fredericton and Bathurst, and MacDonalds from Bras d'Or,
> Night ramps and gallivanters, swift runners and fast canters,
> All work for daily wages round the Scow on Cowden's Shore.

Sic transit gloria. The old lumber towns have long since vanished from the river shore, and the land cleared of timber is now given over to the growing of potatoes. Potatoes have created wealth in the Andover and Grand Falls districts where many of the country homes are baronial in size and elegance. It is difficult, though, to dramatize a potato. It is celebrated in local festivals, each festival presided over by a glamorous queen, but no one, so far as I know, has ever sung the praises of the potato in a ballad.

Above Grand Falls the valley is contracted and the river runs between high hills. In its upper reaches the St. John is not a provincial waterway but an international boundary separating New Brunswick from Maine. The separation is more geographical than political, for the boundary is hardly recognized as such by the people living on either shore, and the customs houses seem to exist only to catch tourists.

Here above Grand Falls the people are nearly all French-speaking Acadians, quieter, less volatile, less self-consciously a race apart than their Quebec brethren. The church-dominated towns – St. Leonard,

67

Ste. Anne, Rivière Verte – look weather-beaten and depressed by comparison with the down-river English-speaking communities, but their citizens are seemingly content with the *status quo*. Edmundston, the last New Brunswick town of consequence on the Highway, is a busy pulp-and-paper centre at the junction of the St. John and Madawaska rivers, and the home of the first French-speaking premier of New Brunswick. Edmundston provides a fine example of international industrial co-operation; wood ground into pulp in an Edmundston plant is piped across the river and made into sulphite in a plant on the American side.

The valley of the St. John – and, indeed, all of New Brunswick – is widely advertised as a sportsman's paradise. I am not myself a sportsman. I take no pleasure in huddling in a muddy pit through a cold and windy dawn on the off-chance of filling an innocent bird full of buck-shot; nor do I look on death through being mistaken for a moose as of all deaths the most honourable. A fish, if he fails to rise to my first cast, is thereafter safe, for I will spend the rest of the day trying to disentangle my line from reel or near-by tree. But the valley of the St. John is a region where rod and gun lie ready to the hand of every citizen, and no doubt with reason. One of the great days of my life I spent carrying a gun through the New Brunswick woods when the hills above the river were on fire with the flames of autumn and the river the intensest sapphire blue I have ever seen. To add to the day's beauty no bird rose to challenge my marksmanship, and I was spared the pain of striking down out of vanity something I really preferred to let live, or the embarrassment of a clean miss.

I feel strongly, though, that those who publicize New Brunswick's hunting and fishing attractions should coin a new slogan. 'Sportsman's Paradise' now means any community in North America possessing a pond, a duck or two, and a Chamber of Commerce.

The Atlantic provinces are homogeneous in that all four are sea-girt, heavily populated along their coasts, and sparsely populated in their forested interiors. And all four for economic and geographic reasons tend to varying degrees to turn away from the rest of Canada and face the United States or the Atlantic Ocean or both. But between

The gorge at Grand Falls

New Brunswick and her sister provinces there is a significant difference. Newfoundland, Prince Edward Island, and Nova Scotia are islands (the Chignecto Isthmus is an accident which hardly affects Nova Scotia's island mentality); but New Brunswick is unequivocally a piece of the continent, a part of the main. Geography has forced upon her an acceptance of her destiny; and outsiders find among the people of New Brunswick a greater awareness of national, as opposed to merely regional, identity than is apparent elsewhere in the Maritimes.

The Highway leaves the St. John Valley at Edmundston and runs north-west towards Quebec. Beside it the Madawaska River flows south to join the St. John. The Madawaska is a river famous in the lumbering history of New Brunswick; but long before the days of the lumberman it was a French communication route between Canada and Acadia, and before the white men came an Indian highway from the St. Lawrence to the St. John.

It is fitting that the new highway and the old should make their way side by side through the dark forest.

River, Rock, and Ville Marie

QUEBEC

The St. John River is a woman and the St. Lawrence is a god. No one can look upon that mighty flood of water, nearly fifteen miles from shore to shore, which bursts into view from the Highway above Rivière du Loup and feel an emotion more intimate than awe. Nor is it possible to associate with the St. Lawrence an attribute as warmly human as sex. In its upper reaches the river cohabits with the land; but below Quebec City it detaches itself from the intimacies of shore life and becomes an inland sea carrying indifferently fishing smacks and ocean liners upon its great waters. Bordered on the north by the upthrust of the Laurentians and the dark pillars of the Saguenay, the St. Lawrence at Rivière du Loup is invested with an intimidating grandeur which denies affection and inspires adoration.

It is no doubt absurd to assume knowledge of a region merely because we have dashed through it at a mile a minute, interrupting our progress by an occasional frantic slewing-out of the traffic line for a split-second look at the view. But the truth is that sometimes a glimpse of a plain or river or mountain caught in the lightning's flash imprints itself on the mind with an intensity which a prolonged association never achieves — as if for that fleeting moment the curtain was drawn on eternity and we see things normally invisible to mortal sight, hence all the more dearly to be cherished. (Sir Galahad, I am sure, was more deeply stirred by that first, far-off glimpse of the Holy Grail than by any later close-up view.) So it is that although I have seen the St. Lawrence at Rivière du Loup twice only, and then fleetingly, the view from the heights is imprinted on my mind's eye with a vividness and splendour matched only by equally brief

71

glimpses of certain parts of the Newfoundland coastline, and the haze-shrouded islands of the Gulf of Georgia.

No doubt the intensity of the impact is heightened by two factors not directly related to the river as a natural phenomenon – the relative dullness of the seventy-mile drive through heavy forest from the New Brunswick border to Rivière du Loup (dullness relieved by occasional fine views of Lake Temiscouata) and the knowledge that the St. Lawrence is extraordinarily rich in historic associations. The spirit of the past is easy to evoke here, for the river abounds in memorials of the men it bore on its surface long ago – the explorers, the merchants, the adventurers, the men of God, and the soldiers in blue coats and the soldiers in red coats who came at last face to face in a field beside the city of Quebec.

The innocent traveller who trusts the appearance of road-maps often finds himself grievously deceived; roads which on the map seem to follow a scenic route along a river or lakeshore may in actual fact cut a dreary course a mile or two inland from the shore-line and provide no more than occasional tantalizing glimpses of the wonders the traveller has hoped and expected to see. But the Trans-Canada Highway from Rivière du Loup to Quebec City practises no such deceptions. The river is nearly always in full view, the villages on the foreshore – Kamouraska, St. Denis, Ste. Anne de la Pocatière, St. Jean Port Joli (home of the famous wood-carving family, the Bourgaults) and a score of others – satisfy the outlander's romantic no-

tions of what French-Canadian villages *ought* to look like; and on the north shore the Laurentians form a perfect back-drop for the foreground grouping of village, farm, and river. The view is particularly impressive looking across the eastern tip of the Island of Orleans to the point where Cape Tourmente lifts its rocky face 2,000 feet above the river.

We drove from the south shore of the river across the great Quebec Bridge into Quebec City on a day of appalling heat and humidity, got lost in the narrow, twisting, semi-vertical streets — the natives say that if you can drive their streets you can drive anywhere in the world — and, ill-tempered and in poor physical condition, eventually reached our rooms on the third floor of a fine old house on Ste. Geneviève Street. We rested for an hour, then conscientiously went forth to sightsee instead of seeking the dim coolness of a tavern as any sensible couple would have done. We stumbled down a thousand steep steps into the Lower Town, huddled in the inadequate shade cast by a low wall near the waterfront, and apathetically watched the Golden Hawks of the R.C.A.F. indulge in an intricate display of aerial acrobatics high above the river and the Rock. Nowhere on the continent would such a display seem more at odds with its setting. The great rock-face, the grey walls on the rock-rim lined with ancient guns, the blackened houses and intricately carved doorways of the Lower Town belong to no world of jet propulsion and machines cutting through the skies in precision routines at 500 miles an hour. They call to mind pictures of a time long-past — of flashing paddles and full-bellied sails and wagons rattling over cobblestones and men and women in sober garments walking in slow processional towards the church in whose charge lay their hope of heaven. A time when faith, and faith alone, had power to raise us to the skies.

In the cool of evening, following a thunderstorm of proportions and ferocity appropriate to a city which is a veritable Valhalla of heroes – Sibelius-like percussions bouncing from shore to shore, Wagnerian Valkyries riding the lightning – we explored the outer works of the Citadel, that colossal bastion reared at a cost of many millions to defend us from the United States. But the Citadel is no white elephant; it has been splendid tourist bait for generations, and the nation has long since got its money back.

Things haven't changed much around the Citadel in the past hundred years. Henry David Thoreau with his good friend William Ellery Channing visited Quebec in 1850 and was conducted over the fortress by a young soldier of a Highland regiment. The appearance of a Highlander on an alien rock far from his native land drew from Thoreau a characteristically trenchant comment: 'He told us he had been here about three years, and had formerly been stationed at Gibraltar. As if his regiment, having perchance been nestled amid the rocks of Edinburgh Castle, must flit from rock to rock thenceforth over the earth's surface, like a bald eagle or other bird of prey, from eyrie to eyrie.'

Today bored warriors of the Royal 22nd Regiment, the 'Van Doos', clump back and forth in front of sentry-boxes for the benefit of tourists, and their bright red uniforms add an appropriate touch of colour to the anachronistic display of pomp and circumstance.

There is no other city in North America remotely like Quebec, and few like it anywhere in the world. It is the only walled city on the continent north of Mexico, but its individuality derives not from its walls but from a combination of highly distinctive elements, animate and inanimate, including that most magnificent of hostelries, the Château Frontenac, the clear-cut division of the city into Upper and Lower towns, the marvellous old grey-black houses of the Lower Town which from above look like cardboard cut-outs, the pretty girls who are not quite like pretty girls anywhere else, the Rock, the river, and the great dead.

The great dead. Few cities on this continent contain within their bounds the dust of so much greatness. There are memorials everywhere in Quebec and they are rarely to mediocrity.

'Upon this rock I will build my church,' Our Lord said unto Peter. 'Upon this rock I will build my city,' Champlain said to himself.

Church and city seem equally durable. There is no softness about Quebec — about her appearance, her history, her people. All three are cast in the grand scale.

Champlain's struggle to realize his dream against the indifference of old France, the hostility of the fur-traders (to whom colonization was anathema), the raids of English free-booters, and the ever-present menace of the Iroquois is one of the authentic epics of our history. In 1608 Champlain arrived at Cape Diamond with twenty-seven colonists and immediately established a Habitation — a few wooden buildings surrounded by a palisade — on the river-shore in the shadow of the towering Rock. Later he built a small fort on the Rock itself; and that admirable apothecary, Louis Hébert, cleared a bit of land on which he grew corn and fruit and thereby became Canada's first farmer. But twenty years after the building of the Habitation, Champlain could number only sixty-five souls in his colony, and they were still almost wholly dependent for survival on the supply ships from France. Champlain was undismayed. He loved Quebec more than any other place on earth and it never occurred to him to abandon it. And there in 1635 he died, perhaps dreaming in his last hour not of the celestial city of the Apocalypse but of a mighty rock-bound fortress guarding the colonial empire he had helped to build for France.

Strong men followed Champlain. Men such as Jean Talon, wisest administrator in the history of the colony; Monseigneur de Laval, Vicar Apostolic of New France and later Bishop of Quebec, an in-

flexible, bloodless ascetic who wore a hair-shirt, lived on a diet of porridge and water, and for fifty years fought for the glory of God and the power of the Church against the secular will; and Frontenac the Governor, arrogant, ill-tempered, and brave, who introduced an element of hot-blooded humanity among these creatures of ice-water and iron. Frontenac quarrelled fiercely and endlessly with Bishop Laval, in 1690 successfully defied the guns and vastly superior forces of the Englishman Phips, led an expedition against the Iroquois when he was seventy-seven years old, and died the same year uttering 'all the sentiments of a true Christian'.

Frontenac would have approved the hotel which bears his name. Like him, the Château is massive and awe-inspiring. You are aware of the Château from the moment you enter the city – just as in the old days you were aware of the Governor.

After Frontenac, the Marquis de Montcalm and General James Wolfe.

Of all the many memorials in Quebec City to the two great soldiers, the simplest and most impressive is the granite shaft standing in the Governor's Garden near the Château Frontenac and bearing the inscription:

MORTEM VIRTUS COMMUNEM

FAMAM HISTORIA

MONUMENTUM POSTERITAS

DEDIT

(Valour gave them one death, history one fame, posterity one monument.) Even Thoreau, a hard man to please in matters of language, approved the inscription. 'I got out of the esplanade and read the well-known inscription on Wolfe's and Montcalm's monument, which for saying much in little, and that to the purpose, undoubtedly deserved the prize.'

In 1775 Quebec was besieged for the last time. By the fall of the year all the settlements along the St. Lawrence with the exception of Quebec were in the hands of the American revolutionaries; and in the winter-time two American armies under the command of General Montgomery – fresh from his capture of Montreal – and Benedict Arnold invested the great fortress. Governor Sir Guy Carleton, snug inside the city with strong forces and ample supplies, waited for his ally winter to dispose of the enemy. He did not wait in vain. The Americans made one costly, foolish night attack in a blinding snowstorm — Montgomery was killed, Arnold wounded — and thereafter died quietly outside the walls of cold, dysentery, and smallpox. When a British fleet arrived off Quebec in early spring the Americans abandoned their supplies and fled.

The average Canadian accepts without much question the old jibe that Canada is a country without heroes. But let him spend a day or two in Quebec City and he will say with Pericles that the whole earth is the sepulchre of famous men.

In a morning made cool and invigorating by the savage storm of the previous afternoon we drove east for several miles through crazy winding streets, crossed the St. Charles River below its junction with the Liart (where Cartier is said to have established his winter settlement in 1535), followed Highway No. 15 through the town of Montmorency, and came at last to Montmorency Falls — 150 feet higher than Niagara and about half a mile narrower. I am not often greatly stirred by the spectacle of falling water but I am prepared to acknowledge that the Montmorency waterfall is graceful, feathery, and altogether pleasing to the eye. Unfortunately, power-plants, factories, slag heaps, and tourist debris seriously blemish the charms of what in an earlier time must have been an authentic beauty spot. In the garrison days of a century or so ago the woods in the vicinity of the falls were a tracery of well-trodden walks; and in winter-time the young ladies and gentlemen of Quebec delighted to drive out by sleigh from the city and spend an invigorating afternoon sliding down the great ice-cap at the foot of the falls.

To those of us of romantic disposition and tender heart the most interesting property of the falls is the elegant white house standing close to the water's edge where for three years Edward, Duke of Kent, spent his summers with his beloved, Madame Julie St. Laurent. (Edward had a fine taste in women and houses; his city house on St. Louis Street near the Château, still in a splendid state of preservation, is one of the handsomest in Quebec.) Edward crops up frequently in our history books; he was for some years attached to His Majesty's forces in America and gave his name to the province

of Prince Edward Island. Madame Julie St. Laurent, a fair widow
to whom he became attached while doing garrison duty at Gibraltar, was a lady of great charm and goodness of heart and it is impossible to consider her ultimate fate without some feelings of regret.
Ambition and a strong sense of duty impelled the Duke, after twenty-
seven years of happiness with Julie, to marry a stout, bustling Ger-
man princess in the hope of producing a legitimate heir to the
British throne. (The seven sons of George III were virile men but
unfortunately their numerous offspring had all been born the wrong
side of the blanket.) In 1819 Edward sired the Princess of Wales
(later Queen Victoria) and died the following year from getting
his feet wet.

Lytton Strachey reports in his biography of Queen Victoria – in
which he is neither kind nor just to Edward and Julie – that 'the
subsequent history of Madame St. Laurent has not transpired'. But
rumour hints that she spent the last years of her life in a convent. If
the rumour is true, let us hope that she retired to the convent not to
repent but to rest. She gave Edward more years of happiness than
any man has a right to expect – or Edward deserved – and she kept
his socks dry. She was kind and complaisant and loving (she bore
him twelve children) and without guile. Madame Julie St. Laurent
was no Pompadour or Du Barry; she was a charming, oddly innocent woman, and in everything except name a good and faithful
wife.

There are places in heaven and earth – a very few – which epitomize
harassed mankind's dreams of bucolic bliss, of living close to the soil
(without having to work it) amid the drowsy hum of bees and the
rich scent of clover and honeysuckle; nourished on the fruits of the
good earth (close at hand for the plucking) and permanently drunk
on the aroma of apple-cider. Elysium is such a place, and Avilion
and Arcadia and the Island of the Blest and perhaps Prince Edward
Island. Certainly the Island of Orleans. Above all the Island of Orleans.

Sober, statistics-bound men tell me that the winters are cold, the
snowfall heavy, the growing season less than half the year – but they
haven't visited the island in midsummer. Midsummer is lotus time.

'The warm airs lull us – blowing lowly,' and winter is an almost-forgotten dream.

It is said that when Jacques Cartier's sailors – obviously men with a sound grounding in the classics – first saw the island (then overgrown with luscious wild grapes) they called it the Isle of Bacchus. Cartier's final choice of name was the result of unfortunate second thoughts.

Driving around the island on a fine summer's day over the narrow paved perimeter road is an ideal way to observe rural Quebec in miniature. Across the river on the north shore the pattern of land-division reveals itself with startling clarity. The farms, laid out according to the old seigniorial system, run down in long, narrow strips from the base of the Laurentians to the water-front. Villages, among them Ste. Anne de Beaupré of the famous shrine, dot the north shore; from the island they look clean and white and secure, huddled under the protecting flanks of the towering churches. The island farms follow the pattern of those on the mainland; they slope down to the river from the wooded spine of the island, and every farm has its water frontage, pasture, cultivated fields, and wood-lot.

The island farms are old (some of them have been held by the same families for 300 years) and most of the buildings are in the tradition of the *ancien régime*; the stone houses are pure Norman in

design, except that the slope of the dormer-studded roof is heightened to cope with the winter snows, and most of the houses and barns are painted white, with red or marine-blue trim. The buildings are spacious, immaculate, and surrounded by yards overrun with the produce of sound husbandry – chickens, ducks, pigs, cows, and children. The fields we drove past were burdened with the promise of early and rich fruition; they are the only fields I have ever seen which actually looked *pregnant*. Already the strawberries, acres and acres of them, were ripe, and the plots were dotted with pickers. But no one seemed in a mad rush to fill his basket, and to a Westerner like myself accustomed to the tensions and feverish exertions attendant upon a prairie harvest the pace of life in the island fields looked indecently leisurely and relaxed. We seemed suddenly to have entered upon a world in which time had stood still for centuries and the workers were keeping pace with time.

Our impression was not, of course, entirely accurate. In material things the Island of Orleans has progressed rather faster than the rest of rural Quebec. In the last few decades tractors and automobiles have replaced the splendid ox-teams that Horatio Walker loved to paint; and although a few of the older berry-pickers we saw might have posed for Walker – or Millet – it was clear that the serpent had entered the Garden; for many of the girls wore shorts (with an air), and the devil danced in their dark eyes.

There are many old houses on the Island of Orleans which are a joy to behold and no doubt comfortable to live in; and at least three village churches – Ste. Famille, St. Pierre, and St. François – are centuries old and demand the attention of all fanciers of ecclesias-

tical architecture and decoration. But the one building which lives
in my memory above all others was a small white cottage, architecturally without distinction, standing on the outskirts of a typical,
church-dominated village near the eastern end of the island. A cottage overrun by rambler roses, palisaded by hollyhocks, and huddled
in the shelter not of a church buttress but of a lofty flagpole, from the
top of which a Union Jack the size of a horse-blanket snapped de-
fiantly in the breeze. A small English car, a Morris Minor, sat in the
driveway. The owner of the cottage was nowhere in sight but he was
easy to visualize: red-faced, tweedy, sitting four-square in the back
garden reading *Punch* or *The Times*, a brandy-and-soda at his elbow, shot-gun close at hand – to shoot pheasants or Frenchmen according to season and need. Or perhaps a woman, widow of an old
army man, also tweedy, corseted, addicted to gardening in sun-
bonnet and gauntlets, and resolute to maintain standards among
lesser breeds without the law. But we remembered that an Englishman's home is his castle and did not intrude on the owner's privacy.
Besides, I did not want to risk spoiling the image of him which I had
created.

Beyond the eastern end of the island the St. Lawrence bursts free
of the Quebec narrows and spreads itself comfortably to a width of
seven or eight miles. The north shore is dominated by the splendid
dark face of Cape Tourmente, most famous of river marks to the
early *voyageurs*, and the glorious back-drop of the Laurentians. The
south shore, clearly visible across several miles of water, is softer, less
dramatic – an admirable foil to its rugged northern opposite. The
channel for ocean-going ships runs between the island and the south
shore, and the day we visited the island we saw one of the great white
C.P.R. boats, the *Empress of England*, inward bound for Quebec
and Montreal.

Artists have been visiting and painting the Island of Orleans for a
hundred years or more, but not many of their canvases have survived. Towards the end of the nineteenth century romantic young
disciples of the French impressionists established studios on the island
and painted landscapes which looked like bad Manets and Monets.
Members of the Group of Seven arrived in the early thirties and
complained that everything on the island was so picturesquely ar-

ranged that though there was much to copy there was nothing to paint.

Horatio Walker, the island's one celebrated artist, was a foreigner from Ontario, speaking virtually no French, who found in the island the land of his heart's desire. He lived there for forty years, painting oxen, cows, people, fine old Norman houses, and pigs. He loved pigs above all other created things. 'The pig', he said, 'has never been treated according to his deserts.'

The western end of the island commands an unobstructed view of Quebec City, seven miles up-river. At twilight the towering Château and the ancient grey-stone buildings, projected against a background of fading sunset, take on an appearance that has nothing to do with things seen in the light of common day; present and past merge, and the boat-whistles echoing between the river walls are the horns of elfland blown from ancient battlements.

We returned revitalized from the Island of Orleans to Quebec City and drove out to Sillery to see what is claimed to be the oldest house in Canada. The house, built in 1637 for the Jesuit Mission of St. Joseph de Sillery, stands facing the river on the Chemin des Foulons. The wooden parts of the house were destroyed long ago by fire, and it is probably true to say that of the original only a few bits and pieces of stonework survive. The house, after serving for a number of years as headquarters of the Mission, passed through various private hands and is now a museum. A few interesting items of the early Jesuit Fathers are on display, including several manuscripts in Father Lalemant's handwriting. The other exhibits are of the sort commonly found in museums devoted to North American pioneer culture – old guns, oil-lamps, candle-moulds, hand-carved cradles, bear-traps, moulting Indian head-dresses, egg-warmers, and the like. I was delighted to find among the clutter a gaudy lithograph of Custer's Last Stand, donated by a Mr. Hennessey of St. Louis, Missouri. The Last Stand is said to hang in 60,000 American saloons – courtesy of the Annheuser-Busch Brewing Company. American visitors to the old house in Sillery are likely therefore to feel at home.

I found Sitting Bull's rifle, as I was sure I would, hanging just below the Last Stand. I had already seen Sitting Bull's rifle in nearly every museum I visited in the American West – mid and far – and can only conclude that the great chief owned a gun for every day in the year.

In the late afternoon we walked along the ramparts behind Laval University – an institution which in its greyness and seeming impregnability reflects the character of its founder – and looked down into the slums of the Lower Town – that other Lower Town well off the tourist beat where men and women and children huddle in crumbling shells, travesties of homes where no comfort or peace abides. In fear and fascination we watched a small boy strutting up and down the sloping roof of a house far below us. He carried a pair of drumsticks – probably pieces of broomhandle – and his drum was an inverted washtub placed in the middle of the roof. When in the course of his marching and counter-marching he came within striking distance of the washtub, he attacked it with furious energy and beat a brisk tattoo. He displayed a fine sense of rhythm and if he lives he will almost certainly take his place in one of the innumerable bands we heard performing later that evening in and around the Place d'Armes. But his chances are none too good, for the drop from the roof to the alley is at least thirty feet.

The Lower Town proper can be reached by car down Côte de la Montagne, by foot down the Breakneck Stairs, or most conveniently by the *ascenseur*, a cog-wheel-operated contraption running from Dufferin Terrace to Sous-le-Fort. (My wife and I very sensibly walked down and rode back up.) A tablet a short distance along Sous-le-Fort indicates the probable site of Champlain's Habitation, built in 1608 and long since obliterated.

The market-place of the Lower Town is rich in atmosphere and memories, for it was the centre of old Quebec and here in the early times came all those who played their part in the building of the new nation. Seen under a full moon which softens outlines and creates pleasing patterns of light and shadow the square is a place of haunting beauty. Many of the old doorways and shop-fronts are the work of authentic craftsmen, and moonlight hides the blemishes and tokens of decay. The Church of Our Lady of Victories dominates the square. The name attributes to the intervention of the Blessed Virgin, Frontenac's triumph over Phips in 1690, and the destruction by

83

storm of an English fleet threatening Quebec in 1711. The present church, with its unusual altar built in the form of a fort complete with turrets and loopholes, is a reconstruction of the original destroyed by Wolfe's gunfire in 1759.

The Lower Town is a popular tourist attraction but it has preserved to a remarkable degree a highly individual, uncorrupted identity. There are excellent restaurants and a few sleazy gift shops that cater almost exclusively to tourists; but most of the eating-places and shops and taverns are for the locals, and the only language heard in them – or understood – is French.

The children of the Lower Town swarm everywhere. They play in the square beneath the bust of Louis XIV, on the church steps, in the wonderful old doorways, up and down the narrow streets, up and down the Breakneck Stairs. They are the children of the poor but they look healthy and happy and their energy seems limitless. In a few years the small girls we saw playing in the square will be big girls, and in the evening they will put on their best clothes and ride the *ascenseur* to the Upper Town. And in the Upper Town they will walk along Dufferin Terrace and smile at the dark young men, and they will look healthy and happy and beautiful.

Dufferin Terrace is one of the most delightful features of Quebec City – a boardwalk 300 feet above the water-front running from the Château Frontenac to the Citadel and commanding a magnificent view of the river and the river traffic. At the Citadel the Terrace merges with a second boardwalk, the Governors' Promenade, which extends beneath the Citadel walls for nearly half a mile to the Plains of Abraham. Every evening on the Terrace assemble the youth and beauty of Quebec, a few of their elders, and of course the tourists. But the elders and the tourists don't matter – the Terrace belongs to the young.

Walking on Dufferin Terrace is a ritual as stately and complicated as a saraband, every movement significant far beyond mere surface appearance. The dark-haired, tight-trousered young men walk singly and carry transistor radios; the girls wear their prettiest summer dresses and they walk in bright-coloured clusters – slowly, rhythmically, looking straight ahead and seeing everything on all

Notre Dame des Victoires, Quebec City

sides. Soon the bright-coloured clusters contract as individual parts break off in response to the mating-call of the transistors; the pattern of movement shifts with the choosing of partners; the shadows beckon from beneath the walls of the Citadel and the fields beyond; the crowd thins out until at last the tourists, weary of limb and haggard of face but terrified of missing anything, walk almost alone.

The dark young men who promenade on Dufferin Terrace look like dark young men everywhere; but the girls are uniquely lovely. Their beehive hair-dos are as monstrous as beehive hair-dos everywhere, but they wear their clothes with an air that confers distinction on the cheapest dress, and they know why Eve was created and they walk in that knowledge.

If for a single night I could be twenty-one again I would buy a transistor radio and walk on Dufferin Terrace.

On our last evening in Quebec City, July 1st, Dominion Day, we took part in a splendid festival held in the park adjoining the Château Frontenac to honour *not* the Fathers of Confederation but Samuel de Champlain. It was a wonderfully stirring and mixed-up kind of evening. Thousands gathered in the park and the adjoining Place d'Armes. Silver-tongued orators mounted a platform at the base of Champlain's statue and made fighting speeches about safeguarding the sacred rights of Quebec that no one listened to; and a hairy-chested baritone accompanied by a handful of busbied brass players competed spiritedly but in vain against the noise of a thousand transistors and a dozen quick-stepping bands which poured from all directions into the Place d'Armes. All of us except the speakers and the baritone had a glorious time; and when later on a military band concluded a concert with *God Save the Queen* we all clapped enthusiastically.

Quebec is an unsophisticated town and almost innocently gay. Speeches are fine, Champlain was a great man, and the political and economic rights of French Canada must be safeguarded. But there are other things that matter too in Quebec City besides speeches and Champlain and the rights of French Canada; and long before midnight the speakers gave up, the bands disappeared, the middle-aged went to bed, the old to the taverns (knowing they have little time left and putting it to the best possible use), and the young to the boardwalk and the shadows beyond the last circles of light.

The run from Quebec City to Montreal over the Trans-Canada Highway (No. 9) is one of unsurpassed dullness. There is wonderful country lying on either side – the St. Lawrence shore twenty miles north, the rolling, lake-dotted Eastern Townships forty or fifty miles south; but our road runs arrow-straight mile after mile through dismal spruce forest, and the few villages it touches are without personality or interest. It is a road with a sinister reputation, for boredom and long, straight stretches of flawless asphalt invite high speeds and sudden death.

The entry into Montreal from the east over the Jacques Cartier Bridge is spectacular, and an admirable introduction to Canada's largest and most cosmopolitan city. Halfway across the river and immediately below the bridge lies St. Helen's Island (named by the forty-year-old bridegroom Samuel de Champlain in honour of his twelve-year-old bride) – for generations a pleasant mid-river retreat for harassed urbanites and tired seagulls, soon to be sacrificed to the needs of the 1967 World's Fair. From the bridge the Highway penetrates the city north along Papineau Street, then swings left onto Sherbrooke Street, half a century ago the handsomest street in Canada and still distinguished by its nineteenth-century greystone houses, once the homes of the well-to-do but now nearly all exclusive *boutiques*. The Highway route along Sherbrooke and through the western end of the city is well marked and easy to follow. It takes the traveller off the Island of Montreal at Ste. Anne de Bellevue, about fifteen miles from the city's heart.

One of the many pleasant little ironies about Montreal is the fact that although it has long enjoyed – over the protests of its more sophisticated citizens – the reputation of being the gayest and wickedest city on the continent, it was founded as a religious colony dedicated to the propagation of the gospel and salvation of souls. Champlain had built a trading-post at the foot of the Mountain in 1611, but the permanent settlement was the work of two French religious zealots whose enthusiasm was directed to the New World by a reading of the immensely popular Jesuit *Relations*. They were fortunate enough to secure adequate financial backing for the proposed settlement, and ideal leaders in the Sieur de Maisonneuve – 'my honour obliges me to go there and found a colony were every tree on the island changed into an Iroquois' – and Jeanne Mance, a young lady of chaste life, lofty ideals, and complete insensitivity to physical discomforts.

From the outset the young colony contended with fearful difficulties – shortage of supplies from France, the bitter jealousy of Quebec City, and the unrelenting hostility of the Iroquois who had never forgiven the French for Champlain's part against them many years before. During most of the seventeenth century Ville Marie, as Montreal was originally called, endured an almost constant state of siege. Among the heroes moulded by that savage time, Adam Dollard and his companions of the Long Sault are the best known; but Philippe Hébert's admirable statue to Maisonneuve which stands in the middle of Montreal's Place d'Armes chooses wisely among the worthies to be honoured. Maisonneuve first of all – a man of integrity, courage, and faith; at his feet that remarkable woman Jeanne Mance, founder of Montreal's first hospital and indefatigable fund-raiser back in old France; Charles le Moyne and Lambert Closse, two of Maisonneuve's best officers and fighting men; and the excellent dog Pilote whose talent for smelling out

Iroquois saved scores of settlers' lives in the days when a hostile red man seems to have lurked behind every bush.

Peace came in the last years of the century out of a council between Indians and French at which many pipes were smoked and great oaths sworn. Thereafter Montreal had no one to fear except the English.

Montreal is a difficult city for the casual visitor to appreciate or talk about because its attractions, unlike those of Quebec, are not immediately obvious. Long-time residents of Montreal are unhappy anywhere else; those who know it for a few days only, particularly during mid-summer, are usually glad to leave. The heat is sometimes intense, the noise always appalling, and the compensations not immediately apparent, especially to the visitor whose interests are antiquarian. Montreal is rich in historic associations but there are few tangible evidences of those associations now in existence. Montrealers show a fine disregard of old things: they are forever building up and tearing down; and you live in the city with a continuing sense of unease, fearful of waking up some morning to find that the Mountain has been bulldozed into the river overnight.

The best place to establish communion with the past is the Place d'Armes, near the water-front between the streets of St. James and Notre Dame. The Place is the heart of old Ville Marie, 300 years ago a fort, chapel, parade-ground, and market-place. Today the worlds of the flesh and the spirit still share the Place, their symbols half a dozen bank buildings and the great church of the Sulpicians — Notre Dame de Montréal.

The original church of the colony was a log chapel built in 1642. The Seminary of St. Sulpice, part of which still stands, was begun in 1663. The present church, an immense structure capable of accommodating 15,000 people, was completed in 1829. The Sulpicians are a wealthy order owning vast properties in Montreal; inside the church (whose exterior is rather austere and forbidding) evidences of their wealth are to be found in the elaborate ornamentation and extensive and intricate wood-carving. But the priest who showed us around the church seemed only perfunctorily interested in the ornaments and tapestries and wood-carving. He was a faded little man, serene, child-like, no longer much concerned about things of the world. 'You are not Catholics? No — no — of course not. But it does not matter — not at all. All children of God — children of God.' His love was not for the church building but for the Seminary garden behind it, which he showed us with the eagerness of a child uncovering a cherished secret. 'We are in the country here — you see? In the heart of a great city — yes — but in the country. No noise — no noise at all. And we hear the birds sing in the morning. They sing so beautifully — God's creatures . . . '

We were greatly pleased with the old priest, for we had not expected to find a St. Francis in Montreal.

And we were pleased with the Sulpicians. The central home of the Order is the huge college on Sherbrooke Street, begun as the Mountain Mission in 1676. The towers of the original fort, now nearly 300 years old, still stand in the college grounds. And in those grounds we parked our car during our stay in Montreal. The Sulpicians are wealthy, but whether out of simple kindness or the conviction that great oaks from little acorns grow and if you look after the pennies the pounds will take care of themselves, they rent part of the college grounds as tourist-house parking space. Few experiences during our stay in Montreal gave us greater pleasure — after a day of fierce competitive driving, once or twice against the flow of oncoming traffic on a one-way street — than to make a quick middle-of-the-block turn off Sherbrooke Street, pop through an unobtrusive hole in a stone wall, and find ourselves in a quiet, uncluttered world a hundred miles and a century away from the madhouse outside the wall.

The Château de Ramezay, said to be the oldest house in Montreal, stands on Notre Dame Street three blocks east of Place d'Armes. The Château was built in 1705 by Claude de Ramezay, governor of Montreal from 1703 to 1725, as a fortress in miniature against possible enemies and as a home for his beautiful young bride. No doubt military and domestic architecture are difficult to combine, but though the Château is ponderous and uninspired in appearance its history is lively enough. General Montgomery set up his headquarters there after his capture of Montreal in 1775; and to the Château came three American representatives of the Continental

Congress to plead for French-Canadian participation in the war against Great Britain. One of the American representatives was Benjamin Franklin. As might have been expected of an old newspaper man, Franklin set up a printing press in the Château and distributed throughout Montreal a bilingual propaganda sheet called *The Gazette*. It is another of Montreal's engaging little ironies that the present-day *Gazette*, perhaps the most stolidly conservative newspaper in Canada, was founded by American revolutionaries seeking the violent overthrow of the lawfully appointed government.

Montreal has always been notoriously careless of her historic monuments. The Château was saved from destruction more than half a century ago only by the intervention of the Numismatic and Antiquarian Society who bought it from the city and turned it into a museum. Recently, various business establishments in the city have shown concern about the preservation of historic landmarks and have saved several fine old houses in the interests of posterity and public relations. An admirable concern, deserving of wide imitation.

Modern downtown Montreal is dominated by the Place Ville Marie, popularly called the Cruciform because of its shape – a remarkably handsome building in its own right and a fascinating experiment in city planning. The Place represents an inspired counteractive to the contemporary urban tendency to move away from a city's centre. The modern city – Toronto and Vancouver are obvious examples – is a study in dissolution, with society moving away from any recognizable heart and agglomerating around convenient, characterless, and virtually identical shopping centres. The Place Ville Marie is a towering office building, and a shopping centre on the grand scale – an underground city below a city, at the very heart of things. The office buildings surrounding the Place and the offices of the Place itself are empty at five, and under ordinary conditions the streets in the vicinity would shortly thereafter be relatively empty too. But the miniature underground city is already a place of endless fascination and entertainment; and although there is still much to be done to enhance the huge street-level plaza – at present a bleak spread of concrete – it is possible that the Place Ville Marie experiment may be a vital first step in the recreation of the modern city as a social unit, or at least in the slowing down of its disintegration into a series of isolated, identical communities.

Montreal is one of the great cosmopolitan cities of the world and you will not find there the unsophisticated gaiety which is one of the chief charms of Quebec. The Montrealer is self-sufficient and incurious and not much interested in visitors – most of the citizens we talked to seemed appalled at the prospect of having to endure a World's Fair in 1967, even while admitting that it might be good for business. They are on the whole satisfied with things as they were and are, for long-time residents of the city, including that urbanest and most persuasive of spokesmen, Hugh MacLennan, will tell you that regardless of superficialities of appearance Montreal has changed hardly at all within the past several decades. My wife, a former Montrealer of twelve years' standing, and myself, at one time a frequent visitor, are compelled humbly to disagree with the judgment of the permanent residents. We returned to the city after an absence of twenty-five years and for no overt acts on our part were made almost at once to feel like an army of occupation.

Language is the scourge to whip, the needle to prick the Anglo-Canadian with. Waitresses, bus boys, bartenders, policemen, shopkeepers, gas-station attendants addressed us in the tongue which is now less a language than a symbol – not of any vital living reality but of a deep-seated resentment which bilingualism in itself will do nothing to alleviate – and received with equal degrees of impatience our replies in stumbling French or forthright English. And everywhere in Montreal fly the lilies of France, and the flag, too, is a symbol. For old France means no more to the province of Quebec than England does, and to France Quebec means nothing at all.

I think that the French Canadians are very Irish (I speak as a native-born Irishman). They are volatile and acquisitive, resentful of all authority except that imposed by a church, a household head, or a demagogic politician, and passionately jealous of a local culture which they perhaps overvalue and never clearly define. They are superficially charming to foreigners and inwardly profoundly suspicious of them; prone to create symbols – language, flags, songs – to express their resentments and aspirations, and then to confuse the symbol with the thing it stands for. And on the lunatic fringe they both exhibit a fondness for planting bombs in mail-boxes.

In the light of history, the resemblance between the Irishman and the French Canadian is entirely comprehensible. Both are blessed or damned by a Celtic heritage, and both have lived for a long time under the domination of a people of alien temper and language. Dublin's Castle and O'Connell Street, Montreal's now beleaguered fortress of Westmount and the lovely reaches of Sherbrooke Street are alike in this, that to the native living in the slums along the Liffey or in the crowded tenements of Lagauchetière they were – and in Montreal still are – the symbols of alien domination and the dwelling-place of privilege.

The resemblance between Irishman and French Canadian cannot of course be sustained indefinitely. The hostility of which we occasionally felt ourselves to be the victims when in Montreal stemmed as often as not from our inability to comprehend immediately and by instinct the ideals and objectives which even the most vocal of our French-Canadian acquaintances seemed unable clearly to articulate. The Irishman, from the day the alien from across the narrow seas first set a dirty foot on the sacred sod, saw his end clearly and expressed it in precise and passionate words. He was a long time realizing it – 800 years – but over the stretch of centuries his conception of the end never varied, or of the means to achieve it.

And herein lies a fundamental difference between the Irishman and the French Canadian. The Irishman is a fighter, the French Canadian – in spite of occasional raids on armouries, and similar aberrations – a man of peace. It seems unlikely therefore that the Place Ville Marie will ever assume the historic significance of those Dublin centres of rebellion and death, the Four Courts and the Post Office.

Montreal is a fascinating city but we left it with few regrets – perhaps because we had been spoiled by our marvellous days and nights in Quebec. When we go back to Montreal it will be in the fall of the year when the nights are cool and the days rich with the peculiar tangy smells of autumn, and the Mountain (unless overlaid by smog) a flame-coloured back-drop for the greatest inland ocean port in the world.

In the meantime we are studying French like mad.

Shield Without End

ONTARIO

Since Ontario is traditionally monolingual, loyal to the Crown and hostile to Popery, it seems fitting that the passage across the border from Lower to Upper Canada (i.e., Quebec to Ontario) should be accompanied by a breaking-out of the Union Jack and speeches of welcome from representatives of the English-speaking Union and the Orange Lodge. But the border between Quebec and Ontario is a long way from Toronto, and for most of the 125-mile run to Ottawa we are still in French-speaking Roman Catholic Canada, with every town and hamlet dominated by its church. Indeed, there is little evidence for the first hundred miles inside Ontario to show that we have left Quebec.

Between Montreal and Ottawa the Highway runs alongside the Ottawa River. In its lower reaches the river loses a good deal of its earlier exuberance; here between Ottawa and Montreal it is pleasantly pastoral, widening at times to form long narrow lakes and graced by the dignity befitting a stream which flows through the capital city of the Dominion.

The Ottawa played a significant role in the exploration and development of French Canada. When the Iroquois blocked off the St. Lawrence River country west of Montreal early in the seventeenth century the Ottawa replaced the St. Lawrence as the logical route west to the Great Lakes. Fur-traders, explorers (including Champlain), and missionaries (mostly Jesuits) travelled up its broad waters to its tributary the Mattawa, portaged from the headwaters of the Mattawa to Lake Nipissing, crossed Lake Nipissing, paddled down French River flowing out of Nipissing into Lake Huron, thence west to Sault Ste. Marie or south into Georgian Bay and the country of the Hurons where the Jesuits worked and died for the faith.

Ottawa is an easy city to drive into and through. The best way to enter from the east is on alternate Highway No. 17 along Montreal Road and its extensions, Rideau and Wellington streets. Wellington Street leads past the heart of the nation – the Parliament Buildings on Parliament Hill, high above the Ottawa River.

In its role of capital city of the Dominion, Ottawa has much to commend it. Since most of its public buildings are concentrated in a relatively small area it is admirably convenient for sightseeing. Government departments are now being decentralized to relieve pressure on the city's heart; but an area less than a mile square encompasses all the obvious sights – Parliament Buildings, War Memorial, Château Laurier, Supreme Court, Justice Building, Bytown Museum, National Mint, Ottawa University, and the National Gallery of Canada (well worth a visit because of its excellent collection of Canadian paintings). Here too on Parliament Hill the business of the nation encompasses the pleasure of the tourist – red-coated Mounties stand ready to be photographed, and a military guard which doesn't guard anything is changed regularly in the best Buckingham Palace tradition at ten every morning during the tourist season.

The visitor who is pressed for time and wishes to make the best possible use of it should go at once to Nepean Point, a small park behind the Château Laurier overlooking the Ottawa and Gatineau rivers and the city of Hull on the Quebec side of the Ottawa. Here on Nepean Point Champlain, cast in bronze, looms against the background of the two great rivers; and far above on the south side of the Ottawa the Parliament Buildings and the Peace Tower are magnificently silhouetted against the sky. Ottawa is a beautiful city; and viewed from Nepean Point it possesses not only authentic beauty but a grandeur worthy of a nation's capital. The river below the point is wide and swift-flowing; and logs sliding down on the current remind us that the great lumbering days are not altogether dead.

Ottawa must be a pleasant city to live in. It abounds in fine

Peace Tower and Library, Ottawa

parks and admirable scenic drives; and the residential sections are quiet and well-treed and within convenient distance of up-to-date shopping centres. But unless we are drawn to the city by special interests such as the Parliamentary Library or the Dominion Archives few of us who are non-residents are likely to be happy in Ottawa for long. The truth is that in spite of its beauty Ottawa is a dull city, and nothing much can be done to change things, for its dullness was ordained by its history.

A hustling Yankee named Philemon Wright opened up the Ottawa country at the beginning of the nineteenth century. He led a party of New England families up-river to the site of the present city of Hull, cleared the land, sold lumber, grew crops, sold grain, and greatly prospered. When he died at the age of eighty he was one of the richest men in Canada. Nicholas Sparks, who once worked for Wright, bought the land on which the city of Ottawa is now centred and made his fortune when that fine engineer, red-faced, black-whiskered Colonel John By, built the Rideau Canal under commission from the Imperial Government, thereby establishing a waterway from the Ottawa River to Kingston Harbour on Lake Ontario.

> A man who knew not how to flinch,
> A British soldier every inch;
> Courteous alike to low and high,
> A gentleman was Colonel By –

But his manly qualities and engineering skills could not save him from the censure of a parsimonious Imperial Government. He was unfairly accused of spending money without specific authorization and was denied the knighthood rightfully his.

The town which sprang up on Nicholas Sparks's land – called Bytown after the worthy Colonel – quickly grew into a tough lumbering community celebrated as the locale of frequent and ferocious brawls between French Canadians and shanty Irish. And in the year 1858 Queen Victoria gave the young nation one of the biggest shocks of its history by being pleased to name Bytown – in Goldwin Smith's phrase 'a sub-Arctic lumber village' – the capital city of Canada.

Bytown, or Ottawa as it had been renamed a short time before, was a desperation compromise choice designed to end the bitter feuding among those cities – Montreal, Toronto, Kingston – which had legitimate claims to recognition. The choice achieved its immediate objective; but in the long run it has meant that Ottawa, like Canberra and up to a point Washington, is inevitably an artificial creation designed to serve a particular and limited end.

The great capitals of the world – Rome, London, Paris – are great cities first and seats of government second. Remove Westminster from London and something is lost certainly, but London remains one of the biggest and most exciting cities on earth. Remove Parliament and all the appurtenances thereof from Ottawa and what is left?

A pleasant small town in the bush.

Present-day Ottawa is a sober, cautious, civil-service town of good taste, good manners, and a greyish atmosphere even when the sun shines. A Londoner carries an umbrella as a substitute swagger-stick, a Parisian as a weapon with which to play Cyrano de Bergerac, and an Ottawan to keep off the rain.

In an elegiac tribute to William Lyon Mackenzie King, for twenty-one years Prime Minister of Canada, our gadfly poet Frank Scott suggests that during his tenure of office King effectively moulded his fellow-Canadians in his own uninspiring image:

> How shall we speak of Canada,
> Mackenzie King dead?
> The Mother's boy in the lonely room
> With his dog, his medium and his ruins?
>
> He blunted us.
>
> We had no shape
> Because he never took sides,
> And no sides
> Because he never allowed them to take shape. . . .
>
> He seemed to be in the centre
> Because we had no centre,
> No vision
> To pierce the smoke-screen of his politics.

Truly he will be remembered
Wherever men honour ingenuity,
Ambiguity, inactivity, and political longevity.

Let us raise up a temple
To the cult of mediocrity,
Do nothing by halves
Which can be done by quarters.

The mother's boy, the dog — these symbols we may accept, for they accord with the image of ourselves which we masochistically create and cherish. Especially the mother's boy. But not the ruins. Here any parallel between Mackenzie King and ultra-respectable Johnny Canuck peering clear-eyed and short-sighted from beneath the brim of his Boy Scout hat breaks down. For the ruins belong to a remote, spirit-haunted world lying far beyond the ken of those of us who pursue the narrow round from home to church to office to the Saturday-night drunk at the golf club (or, if we live in Ottawa, across the river in Hull, Quebec).

Kingsmere is a pleasant conventional country estate in the heart of the pleasant conventional Gatineau Hills, a few miles out of Ottawa and easily accessible over good roads, although for reasons which quickly become apparent the route to Kingsmere is inadequately marked. To Kingsmere William Lyon Mackenzie King, the stuffy little old-maidish Prime Minister of Canada, retired on week-ends to rest and meditate and pray.

And what else?

Consult with strange gods.

The clap-board house, the old barn, the lawns, the flowerbeds are dignified, wholesome, and commonplace. But the spirit of Kingsmere is wholly alien to our experience and not quite sane. Queer things lurk just beyond the fences, in the woods, and behind hedges; dignified ladies stroll across the ample lawns and Pan peers at them from a near-by thicket and fingers his pipes and shakes his head.

The Kingsmere 'ruins' — unfinished arches, bits and pieces of old stonework set in cement (most of them discarded from Westminster), pillars simulating the remains of Greek temples — achieve a degree of incongruity in relation to the clap-board house and expansive lawns which passes far beyond the ridiculous and ap-

99

proaches the sublime. Close inspection of the ruins adds to our bewilderment. Let us admit that the little man in the high stiff collar was a throwback to more primitive times, that under the full moon he consulted the entrails and offered up sacrifices — mangled political opponents? — to strange gods, always being careful to finish in time to occupy his pew on Sunday morning in the Ottawa First Presbyterian Church. But what are we to make of a man who in cold blood erects on his estate the portico of a dismantled down-town Ottawa bank?

The girl from the Department of External Affairs who showed us around Kingsmere — herself a poet and perhaps abnormally sensitive to atmosphere — shivered a little in the warm sunlight. 'If he put up all this junk thinking it was art — that's awful,' she said. 'But if he put it up because he really *liked* it — because it did something to him . . . '

She shivered again. 'My God,' she said.

'For nearly half a century Kingsmere has been my real home. I bequeath my Kingsmere properties to Canada as a thank offering for the opportunity of public service which the people of my country have given to me.'

Few national leaders have left to their people a more embarrassing bequest. How, after all, do we explain to foreigners the attempt of a prime minister whom we kept in office twenty-one years to build in the middle of a Canadian cow-pasture a ruined Greek temple from the door of a nineteenth-century bank?

How do we explain it to ourselves?

From time to time various ladies' groups have made vague propitiatory gestures towards Kingsmere — patched up this, tidied up that — and left behind them little plaques as evidence of their diligence, but clearly no one's heart is in the task of maintenance and Kingsmere is beginning to look tatty and neglected. When we were there men with lawn-mowers and other implements of grooming were constantly in sight but never in motion — perhaps because they felt brisk movement, or movement of any kind, to be out of keeping with the surrounding statuary.

I found Kingsmere immensely comforting. For it assures us that the ultra-conventional little horse-trader who in our more despon-

dent moments we equate with the national character was at times – perhaps during certain phases of the moon – a nonconformist beyond the wildest imaginings of the most nihilistic, pot-smoking pad-dweller among us. If Kingsmere, through Mackenzie King, reflects a facet of national character, there is hope for us yet.

The traveller driving west from Ottawa is confronted by the necessity of choosing between *two* Trans-Canada routes – the Ottawa Valley route via Highway No. 17 to North Bay and Sudbury, or the Central Ontario and Georgian Bay routes to Sudbury via Highways Nos. 7, 12, 103, and 69. (I quote these numbers to suggest the confusion they must create in the mind of the visitor to Ontario who proposes to follow the Trans-Canada all the way through the province. He finds *two* Trans-Canada highways bearing *five* different numbers.) Of the two routes, the alternate up the Ottawa Valley is to be preferred. It is 150 miles shorter than the regular route through central Ontario, the scenery is consistently more exciting, and our sense of history is stimulated by the knowledge that all the way we are running alongside one of the great early water routes to the west.

Ontario

A cairn by the roadside a few miles west of Renfrew marks the spot where an astrolabe almost certainly lost by Champlain in 1613 was found under a log by a small boy in 1867. One or two of the towns along the way, notably Chalk River, site of the great atomic energy plant, are of more than passing interest; and around Petawawa, where the army has appropriated vast areas for manoeuvres, numerous signs call attention to a novel hazard for which most drivers are unprepared. I thought I had envisioned just about everything that could happen to us on the Trans-Canada Highway but had overlooked the possibility of being in a collision with a tank.

At North Bay, a busy town which has battened on the tourist trade ever since the birth of the Dionne quintuplets in near-by Callander, a further choice of routes confronts the traveller; he may drive north-west to Sudbury and there be reunited with the regular Trans-Canada Highway coming up from Orillia, or he may choose another route and go 'over the top' on No. 11 through Cochrane, Hearst, and Longlac, rejoining the regular Trans-Canada at Nipigon. It is possible to make excellent time on No. 11 (paved all the way) since the traffic from Cochrane to Nipigon is light; but for most of its length the road runs through dreary spruce forest, and the sense of exhilaration occasioned by being on the extreme edge of the wilderness – James Bay lies less than 200 miles north and there is nothing in between except forest and muskeg – soon wears off.

The Central Ontario route through Perth, Peterborough, and Orillia (where the Highway becomes the Georgian Bay route running north to Sudbury) is at times excruciatingly dull. Peterborough provides the first break of interest after a run of 165 miles through heavily forested country. Peterborough is a pleasant town renowned for its hydraulic lift locks, the largest of their kind in the world. But the glory of the Trent Canal system of which they are a part has long since faded; and today the world's largest hydraulic locks are used almost entirely for the lowering and hoisting of tiny pleasure-craft.

North of Peterborough lies the Kawartha Lakes district – splendid holiday ground providing you have made your reservations. My wife and I spent an anxious half-day wandering among the lake resorts trying to find a pallet for the night, but were compelled to return to Peterborough where our bad tempers were soothed away by excellent accommodation in a delightful motel overlooking a quiet river backwater on the eastern outskirts of the town.

Peterborough and environs are sacred ground to all students of Canadiana, for it was in the bush a few miles north of the city that there lived during the nineteenth century one of the most remarkable groups of women in our country's history, a group including Catherine Parr Traill, Frances Stewart, Ann Carrington, Agnes Strickland, and – most important of the lot – Mrs. Susanna Moodie. (Mrs. Moodie's brother, Colonel Strickland, founded the village of Lakefield, twenty miles north of Peterborough.) These women, most of them carefully nurtured in the Victorian or pre-Victorian middle-class tradition, came to the Ontario bush as wives or daughters of men who were for the most part family expendables or shabby-genteel failures in the Old Country – younger sons, half-pay officers and the like. They worked side by side with their menfolk in the fields, they created homes out of nothing, those who were married pushed wambling, ineffectual husbands into positions of importance in local and provincial councils, and in their spare time they all wrote like mad.

Here I would like to affirm my conviction that of all our misconceptions about the Victorian Age none is farther off the mark than our conventional view of the Victorian woman – a gentle, inept creature, subservient to her husband and the demands of child-bearing, her cultural activities confined to needlework, cushion-painting, and tinkling 'The Maiden's Prayer' on the piano or singing 'The Lost Chord'. These gently nurtured women who came straight from England to the bush north of Peterborough were tough as whipcord and some of them hard-headed as nails. They displayed far greater strength and resourcefulness than did their menfolk; and, even while enduring for years physical hardships that would have laid any one of their twentieth-century vitamin-stuffed counterparts out cold in a week, they found time to write voluminously and well. None of them was a genius, but several were genuinely talented. Mrs. Moodie's *Roughing It in the Bush* and *Life in the Clearings* constitute by all odds the most significant and literate volumes of pioneer reminiscences and observations we possess.

'You feel at every step', Mrs. Moodie wrote, 'that Canada must become a great nation. Canadians possess capabilities and talents which will render them second to no nation in the world.'

Perhaps it is as well that the dead do not return.

As the Highway approaches Lake Simcoe it enters a world of red-brick, tree-shaded towns and full-bosomed, ample farms which for many of us typify rural Ontario; and the sight of the mellow old two-storey houses, many of them with fretwork trim around the gable facings (like crocheted edging on a pair of Victorian drawers), and all with wide porches running right across the front, induces reflection on the disappearance − and the significance thereof − of the front porch from the home.

There was a time, even within my own remembering, when a porch played such an important part in household living − be it in a sheltered old eastern town or on the stark and wind-swept prairie − that the rest of the house sometimes seemed a mere adjunct, an afterthought, tacked on to the vital centre. Often the porch ran not only across the front of the house but along both sides as well; and it was always a wonderfully comfortable and relaxing sort of place because onto it went all the furniture deemed too shabby for living-room or parlour: the broad-bottomed, splintering wicker chairs (no nylons then to pick), the couches that had long since perfectly adapted their surfaces and springs to the contours of the human body, the rickety old tables piled high with books and magazines, and the splendid enclosed swing-seat across the far end where the Virginia creeper grew thickest. There in an uninhibited atmosphere far removed from the conventions and restrictions of indoor living you entertained the friends who really mattered, drank lemonade out of tall glasses on warm, flower-scented nights, read Conan Doyle and G. A. Henty and Florence L. Barclay and Harold Bell Wright by the uncertain light of the big oil lamp, and courted in the privacy of the swing-chair after darkness fell and the young ones had gone to bed. And when you weren't talking or reading or playing checkers or courting you watched the neighbours on their porches across the way, and never once thought of peering out at them furtively from behind drawn curtains the way we do now.

Nowadays nobody builds a porch, and whoever lives in an old house has either torn the porch down or uses it as a storehouse for junk. We have retreated indoors, to the glassed-in living-room or the darkened TV den or the back-yard barbecue; and with the passing of the front porch a way of life has passed too.

Why have we retreated indoors? Not for the sake of privacy; the monstrous view windows which are a characteristic feature of modern architecture – even where the view consists of a back alley or a neighbour's wall – leave few secrets of domesticity unrevealed. But we need a barrier, even if it is only of glass, between ourselves and a world that has grown too much for us to cope with. Our withdrawal from the front porch is a manifestation of the sense of insecurity that has overtaken all men – a prelude to the final retreat underground into the everlasting night of the basement bomb-shelter.

It is time to reverse the pattern, to affirm our faith in ourselves and our fellow men. Let us once more build those magnificently spacious areas of family living dedicated to comfort and the assertion of individuality – and there will be no need of Home and School Associations, or Little Leagues, or Councils of Women, or carpet ball in the church basement for elderly adolescents, or any of the organized communal futilities that bedevil modern man.

Orillia is a comfortable old red-brick Ontario town with Lake Couchiching at its front door and Lake Simcoe at its back. The ubiquitous Champlain was in the vicinity 350 years ago and Orillia has done well by him. Champlain's statue, by the Englishman Vernon March, which stands in the public park fronting Lake Couchiching, is a splendid mass in the grandiose romantic tradition. Champlain twice as large as life surmounts a granite pillar – it is fitting that he should stand atop a rock – every detail of his costume studied, flawless, so precisely reproduced as to distract attention from the sensitive, finely conceived face. Father Brébeuf and the unnamed trapper who form the focal points of the two groupings at the base of the pillar are, like Champlain, idealized; and again emphasis on costume detail hinders concentration on figures and faces. The Indians

— two on one side of the pillar listening in wonder and doubt to the good father, two on the other making a shrewd bargain with the trapper — wear no clothes to speak of and are consequently the most effective figures of the lot.

But Champlain doesn't explain the unique attraction of Orillia that you feel the moment you break away from the bustling business section and enter into the quietness of the wide sun-and-shade-dappled residential streets. After all, as you move across Canada from east to west, statues of Champlain, however splendid, are attractions of diminishing power. In other respects Orillia seems very much like a score or more of Ontario towns of roughly the same size scattered throughout the province. Many of its buildings both public and private date from the most distressing architectural period in the history of western civilization, the late nineteenth century. The red-brick houses are all too often mausoleums adorned with every species of gimcrack ornamentation known to man (with here and there, to lift up the heart, a flawless gem created in the spirit of a Soane or Adams); the Town Hall is a fantastically ugly brick box fronted by two silo-shaped towers and a recent frame addition that looks like a ramshackle public convenience; and each of the many churches is large enough to accommodate all the saved of Ontario, with enough space left over for a basketball court.

No — neither its buildings nor its location nor its statuary explains the unique spell cast by the mellow red-brick town of Orillia. A spell which emanates from a sense of familiarity, of knowing what to expect around the next corner — as if we had lived here in another incarnation when the town looked much the way it does but went by another name.

And suddenly we remember the name — see it spelled out clear in great big letters on the railway-station signboard. Not the new station, of course, but the old one — the one that was here in that other life —

MARIPOSA.

No wonder Orillia draws us with a power it shares with no other town. All of us have been here before.

Stephen Leacock ruffled a few feathers when he wrote *Sunshine Sketches of a Little Town* — cut unfairly close to the bone. But in so doing he gave the town its hope of immortality. Orillia will change and pass and some day, God help us, be a suburb of Toronto; but the little town dreaming by the lake will never change. It has been frozen into permanence by art — 'forever wilt thou love and she be fair'. (No use to look towards the dock for the *Mariposa Belle* — you won't see her. But you know where she is, out in the middle of Lake Couchiching — excuse me, Lake Wissanotti — sunk with all on board in two feet of water, and already all the fraternal orders in town are sending out rescue-parties loaded to the gunnels with bottles of supplies to ward off the chill, and you know that all the rescue-parties will be brought safely on board the steamer just in the nick of time and that everybody will ward off the chill and the *Mariposa Belle* will be refloated just as soon as Mr. Smith sticks some oakum in her seams and the passengers pump the water out of her.)

Orillia is a nice town. But not a patch on Mariposa.

There is no statue to Stephen Leacock (dead these twenty years) in Orillia's public park, but the old animosities have disappeared, since most of the people whom Leacock hurt are now dead too. Of late years Orillia has even begun to take an embarrassed pride in her most distinguished citizen and to exploit his name. The Mariposa Folk Festival has brought money and riots to the town and laughter from the grave; and Leacock's fine old house on Brewery Bay — did he choose the site because of its name? — has been bought by the town and converted into a museum complete with imported curator. Leacock, I am sure, would have been enchanted by the utterly humourless innocence of the charming young guides who as they show you around the house recite their memorized jokes and pieces with a kind of awful earnestness and are thrown into a panic by an unexpected or irreverent question.

There is little to see in the museum. I liked the library, no doubt because the wonderful hodge-podge of books, all meticulously catalogued, reminded me of my own catholic collection (G. A. Henty alongside W. H. Hudson, Charles Darwin cheek-by-jowl with Ethel M. Dell); but the odd letters, posters, photographs on display under glass or hanging on the walls constitute a meagre and unexciting exhibit. It seems unlikely that Leacock ever thought of himself as a prospective museum piece or encouraged anyone else to do so.

It is a pity, though, that he is not alive to write about his own apotheosis.

A few miles north-west of Orillia lies Huronia, land of heroic sacrifice and dreadful death. Huronia marked for the Jesuit missionaries the end of a trail which the Trans-Canada Highway traveller first picks up at Rivière du Loup: a trail which begins in Old France, leads west across the Atlantic, up the St. Lawrence, the Ottawa, the Mattawa, across Lake Nipissing and down French River and the east coast of Georgian Bay to the region which three and a half centuries ago was the centre of the Huron nation. The Jesuits were quick to learn that of all the Indian people the Hurons were the most amenable to the white man's way of life (they were, for instance, more disposed to settle in one place than were the Iroquois) and probably the most receptive to his faith.

For twenty years the fathers toiled with some success to win heathen souls for Christ. In an age of diminished faith like the present the incredible hardships endured by the Jesuits and their almost deliberate seeking of martyrdom for the Cross may seem the clear expressions of a death-wish, and the final dreadful scene when Brébeuf and Lalemant perished in the flames a fulfilment of that wish. But, whatever our own beliefs, we must salute the Jesuits of the Huronia Mission as brave men who died for what they passionately believed in. 'My God, my Saviour, I take from thy hand the cup of thy sufferings,' Brébeuf had written long before. 'I invoke thy name; I vow never to fail thee in the grace of martyrdom if by thy mercy thou dost offer it to me.' He kept his vow.

The traveller may see the visible memorials of the martyred Jesuits by leaving the Trans-Canada Highway at Waubaushene about fifteen miles north of Orillia and driving west for another twenty miles along the shores of Matchedash Bay to the town of Midland. Midland is the heart of old Huronia. There the Jesuits came early in the seventeenth century to toil in the fields they believed ripe unto harvest. And there in the year 1649 came the Iroquois – several hundred picked warriors intent to exterminate their traditional enemies the Hurons. They came in the early spring when the snow was still on the ground, a time when all properly conditioned Indians were content to stay in their villages, and their initial attack caught the Hurons completely by surprise.

The scenes of the Jesuit martyrdom and virtual annihilation of the Huron nation – Fort Ste. Marie on the Wye River just outside Midland, St. Ignace, and St. Louis in the woods near by – have recently been uncovered and marked by archaeologists from the Royal Ontario Museum and the University of Western Ontario, working under the direction of Mr. Kenneth Kidd and Dr. Wilfred Jury. Ste. Marie, the centre of the Jesuit Mission to Huronia, was strongly protected by stone bastions; St. Ignace and St. Louis huddled behind the traditional wooden palisades. The Iroquois made their final attack just before daybreak on March 16th, 1649, overwhelmed the villages, captured Fathers Brébeuf and Lalemant in St. Louis and took them back to St. Ignace for the final torture. Ste. Marie survived; but later in the year it was abandoned and destroyed by the French themselves, and the remnants of the Huron nation scattered halfway across the continent.

The hill overlooking the ruins of Ste. Marie has been dedicated to the memory of the martyred Jesuits (eight of whom met violent deaths in Canada, all but one at the hands of the Iroquois). It is surmounted by an elaborately decorated Martyrs' Shrine, a replica of the Grotto of Loreto, the Fourteen Stations of the Cross, and other manifestations of the pious impulses of men. But art is not necessarily the handmaiden of piety and most of us are likely to feel more strongly the living presences of the martyrs among the ruins and restored wooden crosses of Ste. Marie than in contemplation of the elaborate orthodox memorials on the hill-side.

A local service club has collaborated with archaeologists from the University of Western Ontario in the re-creation, under the supervision of Dr. Jury, of a Huron Indian village on the outskirts of Midland. I am as a rule hostile to re-creations, feeling that a hole in the ground which we know positively was the original cellar of an old trading-post communicates more effectively the atmosphere of the trading-post than any varnished and deodorized replica of the original building is likely to do. But the Huron Indian village outside Midland is such an admirably realistic reproduction that it silences criticism. Even the original smells seem to have been faithfully reproduced; and anyone with a hankering after the life of the noble red man (*circa* seventeenth century) will probably be happy to settle for civilization after he has poked about the village for an hour or so.

The Canadian, or Laurentian, Shield extends from Labrador to the Manitoba border, and from the St. Lawrence and the Great Lakes north to the Arctic. The Canadian Shield is fascinating country of enormous mineral wealth but there is too much of it. In Canada there is too much of everything. Too much rock, too much prairie, too much tundra, too much mountain, too much forest. Above all, too much forest. Even the man who passionately believes that he shall never see a poem as lovely as a tree will be disposed to give poetry another try after he has driven the Trans-Canada Highway.

North from Orillia the Highway runs through Canadian Shield all the way to Sudbury. It promises much, since it is here called the Georgian Bay Route, and offers little. Georgian Bay on Lake Huron is rightly renowned for its scenic charms, but it lies miles to the west of the Highway, and to leave the Highway and follow one of the many roads leading to resort points is to invite trouble unless you know precisely where you are going and have arranged in advance for accommodation. The traveller who puts his trust in his ability to pick up over-night lodgings wherever he may find himself when the stars come out had better stick religiously to the Highway and adjust as best he may to the seemingly endless miles of rock cut, scrub, and forest through which the Highway slices its way. There are no towns to speak of between Orillia and Sudbury except Parry Sound; and the only spot which invites one to linger is French River where a splendid picnic-site on a rocky bank overlooks the stream down which in the old days everybody who was anybody travelled; for French River was the last link in the mighty chain of waterways joining Montreal with Lake Huron via the northern route.

It is difficult to talk objectively about Sudbury and its subsidiaries, Coniston and Copper Cliff, for they are towns which even at first sight induce a powerful emotional reaction. Sudbury is the site of the world's greatest nickel mine, and a mighty copper and platinum storehouse. It epitomizes within its narrow limits the enormous wealth of the Laurentian Shield, the Canada of Tomorrow. It satisfies our pride in size and appals us by the devastation it has created. Appals those of us who are outsiders, for Sudbury citizens are inordinately proud of their town. 'Wouldn't live anywhere else,' a coffee-bar proprietor assured us. 'Not *any*where. Best damn town in the whole damn country.'

He was a big man with a bellicose eye and I did not question his judgment.

No doubt the people of Sudbury share a feeling of communal pride (impossible to comprehend in Orillia or Peterborough or Moose Jaw) born of an awareness of the immense importance to the modern world of the minerals which they uncover and refine.

And what matter a few hundred square miles of blighted vegetation when a virtually untapped, unspoiled wilderness begins at Sudbury's back door and runs clear to the Arctic Ocean?

Copper Cliff is an impressive spectacle in an awful kind of way. The copper-smelter and slag-heaps are of an immensity in keeping with the enterprise of which they are the culmination; and the surrounding desolation makes the immediate Sudbury environs look lush by comparison. But the citizens of Copper Cliff, like those of Sudbury, seem a proud and contented people.

No doubt the long-time residents of hell itself eventually adapt to their environment.

West from Sudbury the Highway (now No. 17 to the Manitoba border) makes its way through country which — except for a few seedy-looking towns and the occasional cleared area given over to subsistence farming — seems hardly touched by man, a great wilderness of rock and water and forest and blackflies. Blackflies tear portions of flesh from exposed areas, and if you are unprotected and unwary they will give you many days and nights to scratch and remember. On one unhappy occasion my wife and I ate our lunch at a pleasant wayside table overlooking Lake Superior, where the flies lie in wait for the innocent, and it was weeks before we resumed our normal outlines. The wise tourist proposing to set foot in the north woods before midsummer first smears himself with all the insect repellents he can lay his hands on and carries a spray-gun slung low on his hip.

The towns along the way are of an almost uniform ugliness and decrepitude, with evidences everywhere of a depressed citizenry living precariously on a little bit of this and a little bit of that — farming, fishing, mining, lumbering — in the middle of a rock-and-forest wilderness lacking the kind of authentic scenic grandeur that regardless of the economics of existence can lift up the heart and set the spirit free.

And here on the long rock-and-forest stretch reaching all the way from Sudbury to the Manitoba border we saw evidences of a social and economic phenomenon created by the Trans-Canada Highway, of consequences as yet difficult to calculate, but likely to be far-reaching and dramatic. For luxury motels are springing up in the oddest places; and nothing we saw in our journeying struck us as more incongruous than the enormous gap between the pretentiousness of the new motels and the general level of housing in the villages along the Highway. One conclusion is certain: the average tourist travelling the Highway through the long forest stretches of northern and western Ontario will learn little or nothing of the natives and their way of life. He will drive all day, stop for occasional snacks at lunch-counters where his fellow snackers will be mostly tourists like himself; and when night overtakes him, even though he may be a hundred miles from a town of any size, he will find lodgings in a motel precisely like a motel in St. Petersburg or Calgary or Walla Walla. He will be looked after briefly by imper-

sonal attendants; and in the grey dawn he will rejoin the traffic
stream on the Highway and pound along through the interminable
forest at seventy miles an hour.

There are gimcrack motels springing up too – last refuge of the
benighted – but most are in the luxury class and so are the rates.
They will enable the tourist, if he so desires, to hole up for days or
weeks in a northern town and be untouched by the life around him;
and more and more the life of the small-town citizen will be devoted
to catering impersonally to the tourist's needs and getting as much
as possible of his money.

Bruce Mines, fifty miles east of Sault Ste. Marie, attracted our
attention by means of a sign displayed on the wall of the post office
listing the town's various claims to notoriety – among them 'Home of
the Marquess of Queensberry'. Surely not *the* Marquess of Queensberry, the man who lent his name to the rules of modern boxing,
precipitated the most sensational libel suit of the nineteenth century,
and destroyed Oscar Wilde? Impossible.

The elderly postmistress was no help at all. 'Never heard of him,'
she said with finality, and went on counting change. 'Sure he lived
here,' the blonde lunch-counter waitress said. 'Like a long time ago,
I guess. They could tell you up at the museum.'

We found the museum only to be thwarted again, for in defiance
of a sign saying it was open the museum was tightly closed. The
library adjoining the museum was closed too. None of the natives
whom we buttonholed on the street had ever heard of the Marquess,
and after an hour or two of vain searching we gave up our quest
and went our way.

We learned the identity of the Bruce Mines Marquess of Queensberry only after we had reached home, when an item on the
children's page of the local newspaper caught my wife's roving eye
– 'Victorian Doll-House Presented to Bruce Mines Museum'. The
doll-house, so the Canadian Press story informed us, had originally
belonged to Lord Percy Douglas who moved to Bruce Mines in
1896 'to take over the management of the mines'. And perhaps –
though the story on the children's page naturally did not suggest
the possibility – to escape the aura of scandal that hung about his

name. For Lord Percy Douglas of Hawick was the elder son of the
Marquess of Queensberry who had hounded Oscar Wilde to prison
and the grave. When, in 1895, Oscar Wilde was charged with com-
mitting criminal acts of gross indecency, Lord Percy went bail for
him – and was savagely beaten up by his father, the Marquess, who
suspected Lord Percy, unjustly, of being one of Wilde's favourite
young men.

Oscar Wilde was himself no stranger to frontier life. He had
visited the mining towns of Colorado during his first American tour,
and rejoiced in the colourful costumes worn by the miners: 'In all
my journeys through the country, the only well-dressed men that I
saw . . . were the western miners . . . ' – and in their forthright, uncomplicated view of literature and life: 'I read them passages from
Benvenuto Cellini, and they seemed much delighted. I was re-

proved by my hearers for not having brought him with me. I explained that he had been dead for some little time, which elicited
the enquiry, "Who shot him?" '

Wilde would, I am sure, have savoured to the full the comic irony
of Lord Percy's presence in the Canadian north-woods – an aesthete
of the decadent nineties being faithful to his Cynara in his fashion
in Bruce Mines, Ontario. (Where, however, a call for madder music
and for stronger wine would assuredly not have gone unheeded.)

The fierce old Marquess died in 1900. Lord Percy Douglas succeeded to the title and returned to England. He had already mortgaged half his large inheritance to the money-lenders and he squandered the other half in less than a year. He died penniless in Johannesburg in 1920. The doll-house which belonged to Lord Percy's children was left with a Bruce Mines family and found its way to the museum more than half a century later.

North from Sault Ste. Marie the Highway runs inland a short distance from the shore of Lake Superior; and here the pressure of traffic intensifies, for we are now on the popular international 'circle' drive for which Sault Ste. Marie is the entry and exit at the eastern end. This is a world which provides memorable experiences for those who know it well, and for those who are simply lucky. We didn't know the country but we were several times lucky. Once we turned off the Highway, found primitive but adequate accommodation in a cabin overlooking a magnificent horseshoe bay on Lake Superior, and spent a long, sun-mellowed, muscle-relaxing afternoon at ease on the five-mile crescent beach. The water was wonderful; and after an eternity of forest it was a joy to get our eyes laid out straight for a whole afternoon and watch lake steamers drop out of sight over a remote horizon. But the lovely beach was sadly littered with evidences of man's eternal sloppiness; and unless it is brought under some sort of official supervision it will soon be almost untenable.

There were campers everywhere along the beach and one family in particular attracted our attention – mother, father, and six children scaling down from the mid-teens to baby-size. They had pitched their tent on a narrow strip of green between the Highway and the beach, hung their half-mile of washing on lines strung between trees, and the baby in a hammock improvised from a clothes-basket. In a temperature of over ninety degrees they barbecued an immense meal and afterwards sang lustily to the accompaniment of someone's excellent mouth-organ playing. I envied them their carefree enjoyment of what for me would have been a fairly agonizing experience, and regretted the unholy mess they were making of the good earth they were camped on.

In the evening we sat in Cape Cod chairs in front of our cabin and watched the fishermen on a near-by bridge fish until darkness came. They didn't catch anything. Men who fish from bridges *never* catch anything. But they make excellent still-life studies.

The 165-mile stretch of Highway running from the Agawa River at the south entrance of the Lake Superior Provincial Park to Marathon was built at a cost of forty million dollars. The road-builders, working the year round, drove their way through a wild terrain where virtually no trails of any kind existed. They blasted through forty miles of rock, bridged twenty-five rivers, and surmounted hills rising to an elevation of 1,600 feet. The building of the Highway through what was known, without affection, as 'The Gap' was a superb feat of engineering and human endurance. At many points along the route men and supplies could be brought in only by boat or airplane, and supply and transport difficulties were sometimes complicated by problems of morale. Blackflies and isolation do not make for happy construction gangs.

The Lake Superior Provincial Park extending north from Agawa Bay for fifty miles will no doubt some day be a model of its kind, since it is the intention of the responsible provincial authorities to preserve the area as unspoiled wilderness and rigidly limit all commercial enterprises within its boundaries. So far the intention has been fully realized; the park at present provides excellent accommodation for campers and not even a gas station for the orthodox tourist.

Wawa, a mining town just beyond the northern limits of the park, has claims to recognition and affection, for although it isn't much to look at it possesses a mighty heart. Some fifteen years ago it was officially decreed that the name of Wawa be changed to Jamestown in honour of Sir James Dunn. After all, Wawa was an iron-mining town, and Sir James was president of Algoma Steel. But Wawa was a name cherished by the citizens of the town. It was the Ojibway word for Canada goose, and the name of the district harked back for generations to a time when enormous flocks of migratory geese made an annual landfall near by. The new name went up on station and post office, but it never polluted

the lips of a single inhabitant. The village Hampdens swelled their dauntless breasts and thumbed their noses at officialdom, and in the end officialdom surrendered unconditionally. Wawa the name of the town still is and Wawa please God it shall ever be. The huge Canada goose, hideous but exultant, which marks the turn-off from the Highway into the town, is an appropriate symbol of the triumph of the townsfolk over petty tyranny.

Nipigon, at the junction of No. 17 and Alternate Route No. 11 coming down over the top through Longlac, is one of our favourite Trans-Canada Highway stop-overs. We have found a charming hideout tucked away on the shores of Nipigon Bay, and the view from the terraced residential streets of the town embraces the great red cliffs rising up around the bay from the water's edge. The drive north past Helen's Lake up No. 11 is for thirty or forty miles an exciting experience; and there are delightful bungalow accommodations to be found on the shores of clear waters hemmed in by great rocks.

Seventy miles west of Nipigon the Lakehead cities, Port Arthur and Fort William, sit quietly awaiting their destiny. Fifty years ago they were boom towns feverishly determined to grow up in a hurry and confident of their place in the sun. A decade or so later they accepted the seemingly inevitable – stagnation imposed by isolation from the rest of Canada – and since then have been associated in the common mind with grain-storage elevators, pulp-and-paper mills, and excellent hockey teams. But the St. Lawrence Seaway has revived old dreams; and the Twin Cities, at present conventional unexciting towns superbly located on Thunder Bay, look out across the bay at that great rock island called The Sleeping Giant and feel sure that the Giant is about to awaken. A mighty port for ocean-going vessels 2,000 miles from salt water – such is the Twin Cities' vision of a not impossible future.

Fort William is a town with a proud history, but the memorials of her past have long since been obliterated. In the days of the fur trade Fort William – no mere huddle of ramshackle huts but a solidly built village in the wilderness centred about a great hall and protected by palisades fifteen feet high – was the inland capital of the mighty North West Company's fur-trading empire. Here the wintering partners of the company, the men who roamed the vast stretches of the West and gathered furs from the Indians, met the partners from the Montreal headquarters in an annual rendezvous which usually lasted for two weeks. Much of the time was taken up with discussions of policy, but before the meeting ended there was eating and drinking in the great central hall of Fort William, on a scale without imitation in any of today's mercantile transactions. In that splendid first chapter of *Astoria* Washington Irving, who had met many of the 'hyperborean nabobs' in Montreal, no doubt idealizes the scenes in the great hall and the men who made them; but it is interesting to observe how a drunken debauch is made glorious in the light of the romantic imagination:

'The councils were held in great state, for every member felt as if sitting in parliament, and every retainer and dependant looked up to the assemblage with awe, as to the House of Lords. There was a vast deal of solemn deliberation, and hard Scottish reasoning, with an occasional swell of pompous declamation.

'These grave and weighty councils were alternated by huge feasts and revels, like some of the feasts described in Highland castles. The tables in the great banqueting room groaned under the weight of game of all kinds; of venison from the woods, and fish from the lakes, with hunters' delicacies, such as buffaloes' tongues, and beavers' tails, and various luxuries from Montreal, all served up by experienced cooks brought for the purpose. There was no stint of generous wine, for it was a hard-drinking period, a time of loyal toasts, and bacchanalian songs, and brimming bumpers.

'While the chiefs thus revelled in hall, and made the rafters resound with bursts of loyalty and old Scottish songs, chanted in voices cracked and sharpened by the northern blast, their merriment was echoed and prolonged by a mongrel legion of retainers, Canadian voyageurs, half-breeds, Indian hunters, and vagabond hangers-on who feasted sumptuously without on the crumbs that fell from their table, and made the welkin ring with old French ditties, mingled with Indian yelps and yellings.'

Old Fort William was destroyed by the merger in 1821 of the Hudson's Bay and North West companies. Thereafter the fur-trading route stretching all the way from the Pacific Coast led to the overseas markets by way of Fort Garry and Hudson Bay rather than by the longer and more difficult passage through the Great Lakes to Montreal. Irving's final words about Fort William catch perfectly the elegiac note:

'The feudal state of Fort William is at an end; its council chamber is silent and deserted; its banquet hall no longer echoes to the burst of loyalty, or the "auld world" ditty; the lords of the lakes and rivers have passed away.'

We spent a pleasant night beside Kakabeka Falls, eighteen miles along the Highway out of Fort William. The falls, being high and confined between narrow canyon walls, make a racket out of all proportion to their size, and the Kaministiquia River of which they are a part is fast-moving and noisy too. The picnic area at Kakabeka Falls is enormous, and beautifully cared for; it seemed to us the finest we saw all the way across Canada.

It would be idle to hope that an Indian maiden did *not* jump into the falls. Indian maidens of old time were never able to resist the sight of falling water, and on the flimsiest of excuses — blighted love, lost honour, poor crops — they precipitated themselves into it. Sometimes the maiden persuaded her lover — if she had one — to accompany her, but mostly she jumped solo. Greenmantle, the Kakabeka maiden who sounds like someone out of John Buchan, didn't exactly jump into the falls. She led a war-party of Sioux, who had captured her and compelled her to act as their guide, over the falls and thereby saved her own people, the Ojibway, from destruction. The local tourist-bureau version of the tale, and a very silly one it is, affirms that at the brink of the falls Greenmantle abandoned her canoe, swam to shore, married a fine young Ojibway warrior, and lived happily ever after. No self-respecting Indian would have any truck with such a wishy-washy conclusion. In authentic Indian legends the maiden *always* drowned.

From Kakabeka Falls to the Manitoba border the Highway runs through 350 miles of forest. We have covered the course several times and cannot honestly say that it improves with acquaintance. In fact, each time it gets duller. There are one or two interesting-looking spots along the way, notably English River where the fishing is said to be excellent, but there is surprisingly little water to be seen along the Highway and a staggering amount of standing timber. The only settlement of consequence on the run is the pulp-and-paper company town of Dryden which provides adequate motel accommodation but adds little to the gaiety of tourism.

Kenora on the north shore of the Lake of the Woods is the centre of a tourist resort area covering thousands of square miles. The name has no pedigree – it is a composite of the first two letters of the names of three earlier communities, Keewatin, Norman, and Rat Portage.

In 1870 Colonel Garnet Wolseley and his troops, on their way from the East to oust Louis Riel and his provisional government from Assiniboia, crossed the Lake of the Woods from Fort Frances under full sail and landed at Rat Portage. From the portage they made their way down that maddest of western rivers, the Winnipeg, into Lake Winnipeg, and from thence up the Red River to Fort Garry. Wolseley's unofficial guide from Fort Frances was a young British army officer, Captain William Butler, who had already covered the route on his own from the opposite direction. Butler was so impressed by the skill and endurance of the Canadian boatmen with Wolseley's expedition that fourteen years later he was largely responsible for persuading the Imperial Government to employ a fleet of modified York boats manned by Canadian *voyageurs* to carry part of the Gordon relief force up the Nile to Khartoum.

Roads in the Lake of the Woods country are few. It is a world of water and rock and forest, a well-balanced combination of the main elements of the Laurentian Shield. It is a world which is a microcosm of roughly one-third of all Canada, and it is better approached from the west than the east. For the visitor from the great plains, tall trees and great sheets of clear water exalt the spirit and accelerate the blood-flow because they are a combination seldom to be seen in his own land; but by the time the traveller from eastern Canada reaches Kenora he has seen so much rock and lake and forest — especially forest — that he may cast a cold eye on a world which deserves much more than a passing glance. Certainly if the traveller is long accustomed to the companionable protectiveness of hill and wood he should look about him long and hard; for the Highway is about to bear him far away from all familiar friendly things and expose him to the terrors of infinite space.

MANITOBA

Manitoba is always spoken of as one of the three prairie provinces, but the Laurentian Shield does not terminate tidily at the border. Western Ontario and eastern Manitoba form a homogeneous land-mass; and the Highway continues for a hundred miles or more through rock and forest muskeg, skirting on its way the south-east corner of the Whiteshell Forest Reserve, a recreational area of some 1,500 square miles which is now being developed as a vast provincial playground and tourist attraction. Falcon Lake lying alongside the Highway just inside the eastern border is so far the showpiece of the reserve. Around its shores are to be found all the amenities — camp-sites, picnic-grounds, golf course, motels, restaurants — which are rapidly becoming the characteristic features of life in the wilderness. Winnipeggers who remember Falcon Lake as a lovely bride of quietness are understandably resentful of what they feel to be the deliberate exploitation of one of Manitoba's authentic beauty spots for the sake of the tourist dollar. But good highways, fast cars, and high incomes invite not only the tourist but the week-ending local citizen to seek out resorts which in times past were accessible only to the favoured few.

The problem of escape from his kind is one of the most difficult confronting modern man. Perhaps the solution is a well-developed back yard and a six-foot fence.

Millions now spend their vacations under canvas; and the popularity of camping out is not determined by economy. Rather, the concept if not the actuality satisfies a deeply felt romantic urge to seek out a lodging in the wilderness far from the troubled ways of men. The wilderness may be an illusion, but the tent at least is real; and no doubt many an urban dweller returns from his camping holiday to the daily round revitalized, and, as a consequence of all that he has endured, a stronger and better man.

My wife and I many times admired the excellent camp-grounds adjacent to the Trans-Canada Highway. We confessed to vague unfulfilled longings at sight of a tent crouched snugly beneath an evergreen at the edge of a rushing torrent; but always we resisted the impulse to hustle off to the nearest supply depot and buy a full stock of camping equipment. The truth is that year after year we have watched various of our friends set out starry-eyed, gypsy-garbed, car loaded to the gunnels with kids, dogs, food supplies, and top-heavy with camping paraphernalia, for a few weeks' cohabitation with nature. And we have watched them return — bleached, bandaged, scalded, peeling, and occasionally minus a toe or two. We are not selfish people, my wife and I; we are content to share vicariously the sensuous delights of sleeping under canvas — parents, kids, and dogs all mixed up in the kind of togetherness impossible, thank God, to achieve at home; of lying awake at night listening to the soothing hum of a DC3 mosquito which, if eventually located and shot down, is in death divided and returns doubly strong to the assault; of sniffing the smell of the evergreen forest through the fumes of coal-oil escaping from a leaky lamp; of rising sore-bodied and sore-headed in the dank grey dawn to wash in cold water and spend a couple of frolicsome hours dismantling and repacking a rain-logged tent.

No, we do not yield to the impulse to buy camping equipment. We slink back to our wall-to-wall broadloom and our posturepaedic mattresses and spend the night in dull and dreamless sleep. And in the morning we rise and eat a dull, conventional breakfast — no half-raw bacon or scorched eggs to titillate the jaded appetite — and after that there is nothing for us to do except enjoy a leisurely morning swim in a heated pool and pack our overnight kits and go.

We are unashamed.

Man has for uncounted centuries been toiling slowly upwards towards the light, dreaming the age-old dream of the oppressed to escape from the cave and the tent and the sod hut and the diet of beans and potatoes and the cold and the dark, demanding a modest share of the material comforts which we feel are the undeniable right of every free-born man. And having won that modest share what do we do?

Go out and buy a tent.

Only a fool rushes in where the author of *Lolita* has already trodden; but there is, I think, much to be said in praise of motels. (Even Nabokov concedes that they are 'clean, neat, safe nooks, ideal places for sleep, argument, reconciliation, insatiable illicit love'.) They are easy of access; they welcome with unflexed eyebrow the most bedraggled unsavoury-looking traveller; and through their design and décor they provide a variety of atmosphere — Oriental, Swiss, Spanish, Colonial, Western, Tudor — which the country they are situated in naturally cannot hope to emulate. Scarred old veterans of the highways may shed a tear for the quaint little motels of yesteryear, each unit complete with pot-bellied stove, broken-down bed, naked overhead bulb, and privy in the bushes out back; and I myself confess to a twinge of nostalgia whenever I observe in some lonely cow-pasture a weather-beaten cluster of long-abandoned shacks and a faded but still decipherable sign nailed to the pasture-gate urging the traveller to Amble Inn or Bide-a-Wee. But the truth is that those early motels were seldom more than rude shelters which sometimes kept out the rain; whereas today's tourist can travel our highways — including the Trans-Canada — in the absolute assurance that if he stops driving for the day at a reasonable hour he may spend the night in luxury and peace.

A year or two ago my wife and I enjoyed a summer's motoring through Great Britain. Naturally we lodged whenever possible in quaint old inns and Trust Houses and slept in marvellous lop-sided rooms dating sometimes from the Middle Ages and furnished with pallets of a rather earlier time. The corridors were always romantically dark and low-beamed, the stairs narrow and twisting, and if we avoided knocking ourselves out on a beam or falling downstairs on our way to the bathroom (our room was invariably on the third floor — if there wasn't a fourth — plumbing on the first) we soaked up a great deal of authentic medieval atmosphere. And then one day in a town in the heart of the Highlands, when we were trying to make up our minds between an inn where Johnson and Boswell had slept on their way to the Hebrides (naturally nothing has been touched in the inn since 1773) and a hotel at the door of which Bonnie Prince Charlie paused long enough to quaff a beaker on his way to Culloden (nothing touched since 1745), we saw just off the highway a most hideous apparition – a row of blatantly pink one-storey units slung in a semi-circle round a gravel courtyard and topped by a huge yellow sign bearing the legend 'MOTEL'. My wife, who was at the wheel, cried out, 'Oh, how perfectly *aw*ful!' and shot across the road and into the courtyard.

The motel was no great shakes but we thought it was heaven. Our room was on the ground floor, bathroom just around the corner, heat laid on to ward off the evening's chill – no gas-meter to devour our shillings – and the meals, served in the little dining-room attached to the motel, the best we ate on our entire trip. We stayed there for three days, resting our legs in preparation for further climbs to third-floor attic rooms. Let me hasten to add, however, that this was the only motel we stayed in during our two months in the Old Country. Indeed it was the only one we saw.

I have only one serious complaint to make about the modern motel: its furnishers proceed on the principle that dim lighting is essential to a truly luxurious décor; and it is a rule admitting of few exceptions that the more expensive the unit the poorer the lights. Some motels are so luxurious (and so expensive) that after darkness falls there is absolutely nothing you can do in them except grope your way to bed. This is no doubt fine for honeymooners and persons of similar inclinations; but those of us who like to read a bit and perhaps write post-cards to our friends would do well to carry about with us a portable lamp.

The Trans-Canada Highway emerges with shocking suddenness from the forest of the Laurentian Shield on to the limitless prairie. The sky billows out to twice its former size; eyes accustomed for many hundreds of miles to looking down a tunnel are unblinkered, and the horizon slips away to a point so remote that it is hard to say where earth ends and sky begins. Some people unaccustomed to great open spaces find the change so abrupt as to feel acute physical as well as mental upset – like a diver getting the bends from surfacing too quickly.

The road runs straight ahead for miles and there are no settlements to impede our progress. Towns loom here and there in the distance – mostly to the south of the Highway and sometimes upside down, for mirages commonly distort the Western landscape – and visitors from the East are surprised (some of them shocked) by the striking similarity, at a distance, between Manitoba towns and those of Quebec. At close quarters the similarity is seen to be dependent almost entirely on the dominating size and position of the local Roman Catholic church; and we are reminded that many of the early settlers in the Red River country were French and that their descendants still live in the territories south and west of Winnipeg.

The traveller will notice, too, in each of the settlements a type of building standing beside the railway tracks hitherto unfamiliar to

him but soon to be fixed in his consciousness as the one that above all others symbolizes the West – the towering slope-shouldered monolith that is the prairie grain elevator.

A pall of smoke obscures the horizon ahead. The highway signs warn us that St. Boniface and Winnipeg are close at hand. And with Winnipeg the true West and the history of the West begin.

Pierre de la Vérendrye was the first white man to reach the forks of the Red and Assiniboine rivers where Winnipeg now stands. Starting from Montreal in 1731 on the first of his many western journeys, La Vérendrye followed the old familiar route up the Ottawa and Mattawa, across Lake Nipissing, and down French River into Lake Huron. He skirted the north shore of Lake Huron and Lake Superior, and from a point near the site of the present city of Fort William traced a route to the western plains via Rainy River, Lake of the Woods, and Winnipeg River. This was the route used half a century later by the fur-traders of the North West Company. La

Vérendrye established forts and trading-posts along the way, and in 1738 built a temporary fort which he called Fort Rouge at the forks of the Red and Assiniboine.

La Vérendrye was primarily an explorer rather than a trader; he was a dedicated man following a dream because he could do no other. His search for the Western Sea ended in disappointment and impoverishment (he spent his own modest fortune on behalf of an ungrateful monarch of old France), and his fame is entirely posthumous, for in his own time he was laughed at and forgotten. Today he is honoured by a fine statue standing in the grounds of the St. Boniface Basilica; and few historians have quarrelled with the tribute paid him by the late Lawrence Burpee, one of Canada's most distinguished geographers:

'La Vérendrye failed in the definite object he had set before himself – the discovery of an overland route to the Pacific Ocean; but he accomplished something much more important. He was in a real sense the discoverer of Western Canada: first to descend the Winnipeg River; first to see Lake Winnipeg; first on the Red and the Assiniboine and the Saskatchewan, if we except the somewhat indefinite journey of Henry Kelsey; first to cross the great plains to the Missouri.'

No permanent settlement was attempted in the valley of the Red River until seventy-four years after La Vérendrye had built Fort Rouge. In 1812 that visionary philanthropist and empire-builder, Lord Selkirk, sent out from Scotland certain remnants of the lost legions of the Highlands and the Hebrides and settled them on a vast land-grant he had acquired in the territory then known as Assiniboia. In so doing he brought to a head the long-drawn-out struggle between the Hudson's Bay and North West companies. To the fur-trader the settler was always an object of distrust and hatred, for inevitably he meant the end of the fur-trader's way of life, and it was clear that Selkirk's colonists were in the Red River Valley to stay. The Hudson's Bay men tolerated the settlement since they had no choice – Lord Selkirk had bought heavily into the company; but the Nor'Westers and their allies the Métis (who were in many instances their kinsmen) embarked on a campaign of persecution and violence which culminated in 1816 in the shooting down of

127

Robert Semple, Governor of Assiniboia, and twenty-one of his men. The scene of the so-called Seven Oaks Massacre is today marked by a memorial standing just off Winnipeg's Main Street a short distance from the heart of the city.

Fortunately many of the leaders on both sides were hard-headed Scots willing to put pennies before pride, and in 1821, a year after the death of Lord Selkirk, the quarrelling lions lay down together like lambs, and the two great companies merged into a reorganized and revitalized Hudson's Bay Company with a monopoly of the fur trade extending to the Pacific.

There follows a half-century of life in the Red River Valley which has in it some of the elements of the idyllic. The Selkirk settlers slowly and stubbornly established themselves, surviving floods, grasshoppers, plagues, and similar acts of God with patience and undiminished faith; the fur-traders went away in the fall to the north and far west and came back in the spring to Fort Garry (built at the forks in 1822) with great bundles of furs for shipment to Europe via the Red River, Lake Winnipeg, the Nelson River, and Hudson Bay; and the Métis, a people of mixed French and Indian blood, lived contentedly enough on their strips of land running down to the river in the old Quebec way, and all summer long were free to roam the great plains beyond the valley where the buffalo grazed in such numbers as to make it unthinkable that they could ever die out.

But golden ages are of short duration in human history. In 1868 the Dominion Government purchased from the Hudson's Bay Company its territorial rights to the huge area of Canada lying west of Ontario. The Métis were not opposed to the authority of the Dominion Government or its representatives; they were concerned to safeguard a way of life that they knew would soon be threatened by an influx of settlers from the East, and under the leadership of the Messianic Louis Riel they resorted to violence to preserve the old order and the land they cherished.

In 1869 Riel formed a provisional government, seized Fort Garry, and imprisoned a few Canadians who were bitterly opposed to his policies. A party of Canadians under the leadership of Major John Boulton, a hot-headed local settler, raided Fort Garry in an attempt to rescue the prisoners, but were themselves captured and added to the number of incarcerated. In a fit of pique or madness Riel executed Thomas Scott, one of the more troublesome prisoners, thereby earning for himself the undying enmity of Protestant Ontario and preparing the way for his walk to the gallows fifteen years later. Opposition to the new order collapsed upon the arrival from eastern Canada in the summer of 1870 of a strong force of army regulars and militia under the command of Colonel Garnet Wolseley, and Riel fled to the United States.

In that same memorable year, 1870, the district of Assiniboia was incorporated into the Dominion as the Province of Manitoba.

It is one of the tragedies of our way of life (and choice of building materials) that few of our cities, particularly those of the impatient West, have preserved any visible evidence of their own histories. The past of Calgary or Edmonton or Vancouver can be recaptured only through documents and records and the fallible memories of the old-timers. Winnipeg has been a little more fortunate. Much of the original Fort Garry was washed away in the great flood of 1826. It was rebuilt of stone in 1835 and of the reconstruction the main gate still endures. It stands in a small, well-kept park in the shadow of the Fort Garry Hotel near the centre of the city. The sympathetic observer looking at the darkened, ivy-covered stones finds it easy to shut out the modern world, reconstruct in the mind's eye a fort perhaps not far removed in appearance from the original, and watch the Indians and fur-traders and Métis and red-coated soldiers of a day long gone pass and repass through the massive portal.

Lower Fort Garry, thirty miles down the Red River towards Lake Winnipeg, is a flawlessly preserved fort and trading-post of the Hudson's Bay Company, and well worth a visit. It owes its existence to the heavy floods of 1826 which washed away most of the original Upper Fort Garry, and to the determination of Sir George Simpson to escape from the unsavoury settlement which had grown up around the company post at the Forks.

For once in his life the astutest of Hudson's Bay governors miscalculated. The lower fort was established, but the life of Assiniboia continued to centre on the Forks. In 1835 Upper Fort Garry was rebuilt, and the lower fort thereafter lived in its shadow.

Lower Fort Garry is now a national historic park. The buildings and walls are in a splendid state of preservation, and it is probably true to say that neither the fort nor its surroundings are much changed since the mid nineteenth century. One of the most interesting of the exhibits on display inside the fort is a York boat, the last of the clumsy but spacious and almost unsinkable river craft which carried the men and goods of the Hudson's Bay Company up and down the great waterways of the West.

Twenty miles north of the fort lies Winnipeg Beach, the city's Coney Island, a well-organized playground and summer resort on the shores of the biggest and bleakest lake in the West. When my wife and I visited the beach we were much impressed by the number

Old Fort Garry

and variety of luxury cabin cruisers we saw tied up at dock – owners
and friends up on deck playing a hand of bridge or poker. One
cruiser even ventured out into open water, but not very far.

The country all the way from Winnipeg to Winnipeg Beach is flat
and featureless; but a drive along the banks of the Red River
makes suddenly real a fact of history which we are all more or less
aware of but have tended almost unconsciously to reject: that for two
centuries the logical route between Europe and western Canada
did not follow the St. Lawrence and the Great Lakes, but traced
its way through Hudson Strait, across the chill waters of Hudson
Bay to York Factory near the mouth of the Nelson River, thence
up the Nelson to Lake Winnipeg, up Lake Winnipeg to the Red
River, and up the Red to the Forks. This way came the men of the
Hudson's Bay Company and the Selkirk colonists and the exiles
from Kildonan who settled the land immediately north of Upper
Fort Garry; and it is easy enough to sympathize with and to a
degree share the feelings of the men and women from the Highland
glens when after struggling for weeks through fog-bound northern
waters they glimpsed for the first time the land which was to be
their home and from which there could be no turning back.

Of Winnipeg it is hard to say more than that it is bright and
lively, with wide streets, handsome public buildings (many of them
faced with local Tyndall stone), an admirable motel strip (on Highway No. 75 running south to the United States border), an ex-
panding university, and many pleasant public parks. The truth is
that most Canadian cities – particularly those of the West – impress
us, if at all, by reason not of intrinsic qualities but of location. Between Calgary and Regina, for example, there is no fundamental
difference, but Calgary because of its superb setting lingers in the
mind of the passer-by whereas Regina is almost instantly forgotten.
Winnipeg is a sprawling well-treed city at the junction of two rivers
running sluggishly between low banks in the middle of the flattest
plain in all Canada. It is a city with a history of permanent settlement
reaching back for nearly 150 years, but except for the Fort Garry
Gate and the St. Boniface Basilica the passage of those years has left
Winnipeg few memorials – a fact which suggests that the impact a
western city makes on a visitor cannot be dependent on time past.

Winnipeg's claim to distinction among Canadian cities rests on the infinite variety of her people. Nearly all the ethnic groups which make up our nation meet and mingle along Main Street and Portage Avenue. Store windows display the names and goods of a score of nationalities; bulbous Ukrainian Orthodox Church domes are nearly as numerous as Gothic spires; and the national division is reproduced in the separation of predominantly English-speaking Winnipeg from French St. Boniface. In the churchyard of the St. Boniface Basilica the man who more than any other split Canada asunder lies beneath a shaft of granite bearing the single word *Riel* and the date of execution.

The Trans-Canada Highway follows the most direct route from Winnipeg to the Saskatchewan border, and it has little to offer of interest to the tourist. (Highway No. 4, which swings north-west from Portage la Prairie and passes within striking distance of Riding Mountain National Park, provides a much more attractive drive, if only because there are substantial hills to be seen in the distance.) Headingly, about fifteen miles out of Winnipeg, is the centre of the old White Horse Plain, at one time Métis country and a starting-point for the great buffalo hunts which provided the Métis with most of their winter food. Here in the years following the merger of the Hudson's Bay and North West companies the half-breed Cuthbert Grant, who had led the Métis against Governor Semple at Seven Oaks, ruled with magisterial powers as Warden of the Plains and captain of the buffalo-hunt. He owed his appointment to Sir George Simpson, Governor of the Hudson's Bay Company, a wise little man who knew that one way to tame a rebel was to give him plenty of responsibility. Unfortunately our awareness that in times past colourful characters roamed across this cosmic billiard table immediately west of Winnipeg does nothing to relieve the drabness of the scenery. Nor does the Assiniboine River, a dismal stream flowing sluggishly between low banks overhung with willows, which the Highway crosses about twenty miles out of the city.

Portage la Prairie, fifty miles west of Winnipeg, is a good deal less romantic in appearance than its name and history lead us to expect. La Vérendrye (almost as ubiquitous in the West as Champlain in the East) built a trading-post on the site of the present town in 1738. A portage trail led from the post north to Lake Manitoba and thence to the great western waterway of the Saskatchewan River. La Vérendrye's sons used the trading-post, called Fort la Reine, as the base of their explorations in 1742, when they probably reached the Black Hills of the Dakotas.

The importance of the post grew during the early years of western exploration and settlement but declined with the building of the C.P.R.; and today Portage la Prairie is a typical, unexciting prairie town, distinguished only by an unusually wide main street and an artificial lake which breeds multitudes of mosquitoes and salamanders.

Portage la Prairie itself may not have much of interest to offer, but a run north for twenty miles over the old portage trail, now an excellent paved highway, to Lake Manitoba leads to a world rare in the experience of most of us – a reed-grown, channelled marshland encompassing hundreds of square miles along the shore of the lake.

The Delta Marsh is a famous wild-fowl preserve, and the location of the Delta Wild Life Station where researchers carry on investigations into the habits, migratory and domestic, of the bird life which haunts the marshes in fantastic abundance. It is no doubt of some significance – which need not be laboured – that the station was founded by an American, James Bell of Minneapolis, and is supported by American money. It attracts naturalists from many parts of the world – dedicated men, for the mosquitoes that breed in the marshes are of a strength and ferocity almost without rival on the continent.

Lake Manitoba has thrown up a ridge of sand between itself and the marshes; and the ridge is dotted with shabby summer cottages and the occasional grocery store and hot-dog stand. Presumably people holiday at the beach in the summer, although how they endure the proliferating insect life is beyond the comprehension of anyone like myself who has been exposed to the ravages of the Delta mosquitoes. Nor is the lake itself conducive to a genial holiday mood; it is a lonely place, communicating a sense of desolation which I am inclined to associate with far-off arctic seas rather than prairie lakes. Lake Manitoba emanates a peculiar chill even in bright sunlight, and the water looks like burnished steel.

The country between Portage la Prairie and the Delta is a delight to the eye. The land is flat, but trees grow to a splendid height here, the earth is rich and bears abundant crops, and the farm homes are no meagre bungalows huddled close to earth but dignified two- and sometimes three-storeyed dwellings, all in an admirable state of preservation and reminiscent of a more leisurely and ampler time than the present. There is nothing that hints at a raw society in a new world; indeed, if the fields were a little smaller and the land a little more rolling a Constable or Corot might happily have painted here.

Of all the provinces of Canada, Manitoba is the most difficult for the outsider to come to grips with. A tourist who sticks to the Trans-Canada Highway and by-passes Winnipeg on alternate route No. 1A may traverse the entire width of the province and note hardly a feature worth remembering. The Whiteshell and Agassiz forest reserves mark the petering-out of the Laurentian Shield; the flat plains around Winnipeg, once the bed of ancient Lake Agassiz in a time following the melting of a mighty ice-age glacier, do not compare in sweep and lonely grandeur with those of southern Saskatchewan and Alberta; the rivers, except when in flood, are uninteresting tree-lined streams which we pass over almost before we are aware of their existence; and the few valleys and low hills visible from the Highway attract our attention not because of their size or beauty but simply because they exist at all. Only the great marshlands lying far north of the Highway and the mighty lakes they border are without duplication elsewhere, and they are not to every man's taste.

But for those of us who feel with Walter Savage Landor that the present, like a note in music, is of importance only as it appertains to the past and what is to come, Manitoba is one of the most interesting of our provinces because of the men who shaped it long ago. A drive north to Lake Winnipeg along the lower reaches of the Red River re-creates as no volume of history can do the sad journeyings of the dispossessed; and a town as dull and stereotyped as Portage la Prairie acquires an interest and glamour which

Brandon or Moose Jaw can never share when we remember that La Vérendrye founded it more than 200 years ago.

West from Portage la Prairie there is little of historic interest to compensate for the drabness of the landscape, for here the only story to be told is that of land settlement, a story no doubt rich in human interest but lacking spectacular events or heroic personalities. Brandon is a pretty, well-treed town in the wide valley of the Assiniboine, and the centre of a model farming district. The town of Virden, thirty miles from the Saskatchewan border, marks the centre of Manitoba's first significant oil development. Donkey engines pump away in the near-by wheat-fields, and even within the limits of the town itself. The results are no doubt profitable but they are also unsightly.

Between Portage la Prairie and the Saskatchewan border the Highway passes out of the old Lake Agassiz bed through the Manitoba Escarpment, a line of broken ridges and hills running from the Pasquia Hills in northern Saskatchewan south-east through the Porcupine Forest Reserve and Riding Mountain National Park to Turtle Mountain near the American border. The escarpment once formed the western shore of Lake Agassiz.

But the Highway traveller is not likely to be aware of any significant change in the landscape — only that he has passed from the great billiard table into a region where the earth rolls a little and casts up low hills far off.

Western Manitoba

Bread-Basket of the World

SASKATCHEWAN

Saskatchewan's welcome to the tourist is reserved, unenthusiastic. Not even a service station marks the point of entry, only a modest roadside sign informing us that we are now in the Wheat Province.

The Highway is excellent, the country dull – a combination that tempts even the most conservative and law-abiding among us to press the gas-pedal to the floor. But no matter how high the speedometer climbs we must yield sooner or later to a sense of utter frustration. For nothing changes. Not the land unrolling like wrinkled parchment on either side of the Highway to a point beyond the range of sight (or so it seems, for a blue haze shrouds the horizon); and not the enormous bowl of sky through which a jet traces a visible line 300 miles long. The Highway curves from time to time for no apparent reason, except, perhaps, to counteract road hypnosis, and no surprises lie in wait around the next bend.

Or the next.

Empty land. Empty sky. A stranger to the prairies feels uneasily that he is driving straight into infinity.

The land is without character. It excites neither hatred nor love. There is nothing here to respond to. Not the austere, sinister loneliness of a true desert nor the friendly security of a conventional pastoral landscape. Seen from the Highway, south-eastern Saskatchewan is scruffy rather than desolate. It rolls not in great swells but choppily, in hillocks and ridges a few feet high; it is trenched by shallow gullies and dotted by tufts of woodland – poplar and willow mostly – which, because they form no consistent pattern in the landscape, create a curious effect of ill-grooming. Here and there a slough (a body of stagnant water) provides a welcome break in the monotony. In sunlight it is an eye-dazzling, sky-reflected blue, at twilight a black miasmal tarn. Many prosperous farm homes are visible from the Highway, crouched secure behind squat caragana hedges and towering evergreen windbreaks. But the deserted farmsteads make the greater impact; they offend the eye and depress the soul. The weather-blackened, two-storey houses with vacant, eye-like windows are reminiscent to a reader of Edgar Allen Poe of the gloom-ridden House of Usher. And, one suspects, many a farm wife of a past generation must have felt a strong sense of kinship with the tragic Lady Madeline: the kinship of being buried alive.

The sense of depression is unjustified; the deserted farms are no symbols of the triumph of hostile nature over man. The land is rich and well-cultivated; given the needed moisture – and its demands are modest – it will produce forty bushels to the acre of the world's finest wheat. But farming in Saskatchewan and generally throughout the West is fast becoming big business. The homesteader who half a century ago reared a family on 160 acres is gone now and his children scattered the length and breadth of the land. The deserted farmsteads are reminders of a vanished, not vanquished, generation. The farms on which barns and houses are crumbling to ruins are probably units of a single enterprise that may encompass thousands of acres. If a marine metaphor may be applied to an almost waterless land: the big fish have swallowed the little and grown bigger. And as likely as not the big fish lives in town and commutes to the farm.

Not even the extension to rural communities of such utilities as light and power and indoor plumbing has checked appreciably the drift from farm to town. Saskatchewan is a land in which modern man finds it hard to live with and by himself. Especially at night when the loneliness closes in and earth and sky assume a detachment and an immensity that compel an awareness of worlds not realized in the light of common day.

Moosomin is the first town of consequence inside the Saskatchewan border. It is a decent, sober place filled with decent, sober people, some of whom live in brick houses – a comparative rarity in Saskatchewan – reminiscent to the Easterner of home. In 1885

Moosomin, although several hundred miles from the battlefields, played a minor supporting role in the drama of the Riel Rebellion. The firebrand Major Boulton, hell-bent to avenge his imprisonment under Riel in Fort Garry fifteen years before, outfitted a troop of volunteers in the town, and after the rebellion was over, returned to disband the troop and sell their equipment back to the townsfolk. But since 1885 nothing much has happened in Moosomin to attract the attention of historian or folklorist.

It would be wrong, though, to assume that the history of south-eastern Saskatchewan was generally as uninteresting as its landscape. The town of Whitewood, twenty miles along the Highway from Moosomin, is today indistinguishable in appearance and activities from nearly every other town of comparable size in the West; but eighty years ago it boasted a community organization unique in the annals of musicology and pioneer culture – a brass band led by an Oxford Classics M.A. (the local schoolmaster) and numbering in its ranks no fewer than four authentic French counts. It is natural to hope that at least one of these blue-bloods played the French horn, but tradition insists that they all favoured the tuba.

In the eighties and nineties the counts cut a wide social and economic swath in the south-eastern corner of Saskatchewan. Haters of French republicanism and victims of heavy taxation, they no doubt hoped to recoup their fortunes in the New World and over their cups plot the restoration of the Bourbons to the throne of France. They were enterprising men of soaring imagination; they had some capital of their own and access to more, and they were spenders on a grand scale. The prairies defeated them in the end and sent them back to France, but during their brief hour of glory they and their lively wives dominated the social life of Whitewood and brought to the community a Gallic elegance and grace which won the astonished admiration and eventually the affection of even their extremist republican neighbours.

Comte de Jumilhac ran a sheep-ranch on the banks of the Pipestone Creek ten miles south of town. He was the biggest and loudest cornet-and-tuba player in the band, and numbered a great Cardinal among his ancestors. He died in his native land as the Marquis de Richelieu. ('Nothing wobbly about the counts,' said one who knew them well. 'They were of ancient, some of royal lineage.') Comte de Langle raised fine race-horses which he always sold at a loss; Baron de Brabant grew and canned chicory which no one in the West would buy at any price. Monsieur Janet assisted by Comte de Seysells established a cheese factory and produced what he called a Gruyère cheese. He was the first to admit that it was inedible. Comte de Roffignac promoted a vast sugar-beet enterprise which

Pipestone Valley

excited the imagination of half Western Canada and failed through lack of funds and moisture. Comte de Beaulincourt lived in the middle of a poplar bluff on the outskirts of the town and painted landscapes in oils. None of his paintings appears to have survived.

As businessmen, the counts were magnificent failures, but for a decade or more their social supremacy was unquestioned. They brought with them retinues of servants from France, they imported the best of foods and wines, and they drove over rutted trails in costumes and equipage — tall hats, white gloves, dog-carts, coaches — unlike anything seen on the prairie before or since. One year they took over the Commercial Hotel in Whitewood and gave a party that is still talked about by the descendants of the guests. 'The Frenchmen invited the élite of the district and some who were not so élite or anything else,' runs an eyewitness report. 'It was a grand success. One would not have thought it possible to scare up so many claw-hammer coats and white shirts and low-necked dresses in the whole country. But they were there. And the French counts were certainly good and gracious hosts.'

Their courtesy was instinctive and without limits. During the

First World War the Whitewood blacksmith went overseas with a Canadian battalion, and when on leave in France called on Comte Henri de Soras, then living out his last years in his native land. To his dismay the blacksmith found the count living in a 'noble ancestral mansion'. But he was received literally and figuratively with open arms, and his leave terminated with a formal dinner in his honour 'to which all the French noblesse of the district were invited'. The blacksmith, far from being embarrassed, had the time of his life. So, one suspects, did the count.

'The gallant and courteous gentlemen of Old France', as one crusty republican old-timer called them without irony, have long since been gathered to their fathers, but their memory still lingers in the Whitewood district like an exotic and gracious fragrance. The tourist who has an hour or two to spare is well advised to leave the Highway and drive south from the town for ten miles into the lovely, gentle valley of the Pipestone Creek. For the valley was the peculiar preserve of the counts, and no one can deny them an eye for beauty. Their houses, amply built on admirable vantage-points overlooking the valley, have like their builders long since disappeared; but near the rim of the valley the Mission of St. Hubert's stands as concrete evidence of the devotion of the counts to the ancient faith (they built the original Mission church), and the valley itself is unchanged. The tourist who enjoys the primitive life

St Hubert's Mission

should camp for a night beside the Pipestone Creek. For if the moon is right and his ear properly attuned he may hear, through the yelping of coyotes on some far-off hill-side and the hum of mosquitoes close at hand, the notes of a ghostly tuba echoing between the valley walls.

Between Whitewood and Indian Head, sixty-five miles farther west, there is little variation in the pattern of earth and sky. The towns and villages, each dominated by a row of monolithic elevators, slip past and none tempts the traveller to leave the Highway. Townsites were originally established along the C.P.R. at eight- to twelve-mile intervals for the convenience of farmers who hauled their grain to the elevators over prairie trails by wagon or sleigh. But good roads and mechanized transport have wiped out the *raison d'être* of half the villages of the West; they no longer serve any vital purpose and the wonder is that they contrive so tenaciously to exist.

Indian Head comes as a pleasant oasis to those who turn aside, for it is the centre of the first prairie Experimental Station (established 1888), and the gardens and trees of the town have benefited from the association. There are a few interesting old houses in Indian Head, survivors of the gingerbread and fretwork days, and the public buildings are handsome and well preserved.

Even those of us who, irrationally, love almost everything about Saskatchewan admit that the tourist won't be tempted to linger on the eastern stretch of the Highway. If he is travelling in midsummer the heat will be intense, and almost certainly he will find himself bucking a head-wind that blows with insistent, nerve-grating monotony from the west. Roadside tables are numerous but they offer dubious shelter from the blazing sun and buffeting wind, and most of the small-town motels seem appallingly exposed. Somewhere ahead lies the city of Regina where the usual tourist amenities — shower-baths, air-conditioning, wall-to-wall broadloom, and cool dark taverns — are sure to be found, and the road to Regina runs wide and straight and marvellously uncluttered. But the wise tourist will eschew the temptations of the flesh; he will leave the Highway at Indian Head and drive north for twenty miles over

Highway No. 56 into a region which seems no part of any familiar world, a region so vast, incongruous, and incomprehensible as to compel the exclamation, 'It can't happen here.'

Part of the fascination of the great valley of the Qu'Appelle lies in its total unexpectedness. I have driven into the valley many times, from north and south, over paved highways, gravel roads, and dirt trails, and I have approached it on foot over naked, wind-swept prairie. Each time, the initial reaction has been the same — a mingling of awe and disbelief occasioned by what at first sight seems a fantastic mirage-in-reverse or a grand-scale hallucination. One moment, we are driving along an ordinary road through a typical south Saskatchewan landscape, level grain-fields on either side, no visible break in the terrain ahead; the next, we are hanging on the lip of a miniature Grand Canyon, in places more than two miles from rim to rim, lines defined with geometric precision, the floor of the valley as far as the eye can reach a necklace of sky-blue lakes, each lake linked to the next by a sinuous slow-moving river whose crazy convolutions persuade us that at times it doubles back on itself.

The valley of the Qu'Appelle cuts a great gash 250 miles long across the face of southern Saskatchewan. It extends from a point a few miles east of Elbow on the South Saskatchewan River to the junction of the Qu'Appelle and Assiniboine rivers just inside the Manitoba border. Like all prairie streams the Qu'Appelle is slow-flowing and turgid — no River of Life shown to the Evangelist, clear as crystal, babbling over rocks; but, to the traveller weary of the plains, the stream and the lakes and the valley are an authentic revelation.

As early as 1780 the ubiquitous Nor'Westers had established a trading post in the valley, and in the 1850s a Hudson's Bay post was built on the site of the present town of Fort Qu'Appelle (*not* to be confused with the town of Qu'Appelle on the Trans-Canada Highway). Indians and white trappers traded furs for pemmican at the post, and there such distinguished explorers and travellers as Palliser and the Earl of Southesk enjoyed the hospitality of the Great Company during their western journeyings. 'The Qu'Appelle lakes may be considered the most western portion of the territory east of the Rocky Mountains into which the Hudson's Bay Company trade; westward of this is unknown, and the whole country untravelled by the white man.' So Palliser reported, not altogether accurately, in 1858.

Following an influx of white settlers in the '70s and '80s, most of them from Eastern Canada and the Old Country, the town of Fort Qu'Appelle grew up around the Hudson's Bay post. Along the valley slopes the settlers built stone houses, some of which are still standing, and within the shelter of the great ramparts they lived lives considerably less harassed and wind-blown than those of their fellows on the open prairie.

But life in the valley was not without its moments of drama. In 1881 Sitting Bull and his starving Sioux warriors, who had fled into Canada following the battle of the Little Big Horn and lived precariously ever since in the Cypress Hills and Moose Mountain districts, rode into the valley for a meeting with the North West Mounted Police under the command of Superintendent Sam Steele. The Sioux sought food, shelter, and a reservation; they wanted to become wards of the Canadian government. But international protocol forbade any such arrangement, and at last Sitting Bull, whose stoical dignity made a strong impression on all who met him, withdrew from the valley and rode back over the border to meet his death, several years later, at Wounded Knee.

In 1885 General Middleton moved from Qu'Appelle village into the valley to put the finishing touches on the training, such as it was, of his raw militia; and no doubt the boys from Winnipeg and the East had a fine time charging up and down the valley-slopes and shooting Indians who weren't there. They left the valley for the long march north — to near-disaster at Fish Creek and final victory at Batoche — when the willows were in bud and the gully streams in full spate. Among the units under Middleton's command was a volunteer force raised in the valley — dashing self-equipped Old Country men under the command of Captain John French, late of the Royal Ulster Militia. Old Middleton at once made it clear that he preferred the society of these 'men of good family' to that of the raw colonials and thereby earned for himself and French's Scouts the lasting contempt of the Canadian troops. But the Scouts fought well enough; and Captain John French died at Batoche, shot through the head by a Métis sniper. He was buried in the Fort Qu'Appelle graveyard on the rim of the valley at a point overlooking the turquoise lakes linked by the meandering river. One suspects that if the dead could see he would have no interest in continuing his ascent to heaven.

Fort Qu'Appelle, built on the wide flats between Mission and Echo lakes, is a town on which age and history have conferred little dignity. The buildings are nondescript and the wind funnels eternally down the ragged, dusty main street, which seems about half a mile wide. But the valley-ramparts rise steeply just behind the town and the lakes stretch into the far distance. Whatever sins abide in the town itself are atoned for by the magnificence of its setting.

The Fort Hotel is worth a visit for its cuisine. In most Western small-town hotels and restaurants food is served to sustain life; in the Fort Hotel it also titillates the appetite. Over the door of the tap-room General Custer makes his Last Stand, courtesy of the Annheuser-Busch Brewing Company.

Five miles east of Fort Qu'Appelle on the shores of Mission Lake stands the village of Lebret, which has grown up around a Roman Catholic mission and an Indian residential school. The village is dominated by the elaborately decorated Mission Church of the Sacred Heart, built of local stone, and by the Fourteen Stations of the Cross straggling up the steep valley-slope to a tiny chapel near the top. The chapel is said to mark the site where, in 1860, the great western churchman Bishop Taché erected a cross and annexed the valley for Christ. Directly across the lake from the village a seminary nestles in the centre of a densely wooded stretch of valley. No visible trails lead to the seminary; in its isolation and serenity it takes us back centuries in time to that bright morning of the Christian church when godly men reared foundations of the faith in quiet wooded places and lived at peace with God and their fellows.

The visitor who has a little time to spend in the valley may choose his lodgings from among adequate motels, indifferent camp-sites, and a variety of rather primitively equipped rental cabins. Katepwa, a provincial park fourteen miles east of Fort Qu'Appelle on Highway 56, is a pinched, haphazard development, to be avoided on week-ends when it is unpleasantly crowded; and the lakes are usually better to look at than to swim in.

My first swim in Lake Katepwa was an experience which needs no nostalgic embroidering to make it brightly hued. My family and I had driven into the valley, which we had never before visited, on a scorching hot, dusty day over gravel and dirt roads. Ill-tempered and filthy, we took possession of the cabin we had rented sight unseen: an authentic museum-piece, lop-sided, leaky, weather-beaten, fronting a gravel-pit. 'Haven't had time to get her really slicked up for you folks,' the proprietor informed us with a genially villainous grin. 'Eleven Montanans slept in her last night.' So, we judged from the condition of the interior, did their horses. But no matter. A swim before supper in the cooling waters of the lake, a many-coloured jewel in the light of the setting sun, would

make all things right. We had a race to see who got to the beach first. I won by several lengths and plunged in headlong. Then, before the horrified gaze of my wife and son, I rose from those cooling waters an ancient Briton come to life, from head to heel a dazzling, indelible blue.

Algae forms in the lake-bottoms in the early summer; it rises and drifts about the surface with the wind. It contaminates beaches, kills fish and even livestock, turns unwary swimmers blue, and gives them the itch. In recent years government and cottagers have attempted to control the algae with a sulphate spray but it seems unlikely that the problem will be solved until the South Saskatchewan dam raises the water-level of the river and thus creates greater movement in the lake-bottoms. In the meantime, the wise visitor seeking exercise will content himself with a round of golf on the pleasant Fort Qu'Appelle course (where a slice on the eighth may land him in the cellar of the old Mounted Police post, abandoned 1884), and a cool shower afterwards.

August is the busiest month in the valley. The farmers begin the harvest then, the Saskatchewan Arts Board conducts a variety of workshops in a group of made-over army huts on the fringes of Fort Qu'Appelle, and Indians from the prairie provinces and some of the adjoining states assemble for a pow-wow on the Pasqua Lake reserve a few miles west of the town. The Indians are readily distinguishable from the fine arts students – their costumes are more extensive and less brightly hued. At the pow-wow these pathetic descendants of the once-proud red man shuffle through the routines of their traditional dances within the shelter of a great circus tent and afterwards refresh themselves with spun candy and pop. The only visible drunks at the pow-wow are almost certain to be white spectators.

For the west-bound tourist the most convenient exit from the valley is by Highway No. 35, which joins the Trans-Canada Highway at the town of Qu'Appelle, twenty miles south of Fort Qu'Appelle. The town stands near the site of an early fur-trading post, and in 1885 it enjoyed an hour of national notoriety when General Middleton briefly established his headquarters in the hotel which still stands on the main street.

The forty-mile run from Qu'Appelle to Regina again invites violation of the speed limit. In the distance the city skyscrapers loom far higher than they actually measure in storeys or feet – on the prairies anything taller than a grain elevator assumes the magnitude of a pyramid rising from desert sands. Viewed across miles of level, dusty plain a city skyline seems an incongruity and, to the stranger from a more sheltered environment, an immense reassurance.

And this, perhaps, is Regina's significant role. It offers the tourist the usual amenities to be expected in a city of 100,000 or more – numerous and excellent motels lining the Highway on the outskirts, two or three first-class hotels near the centre of things, and restaurants where the cuisine is adequate though rarely inspired. But to the stranger it is the reassurance that counts. The skyscrapers may not be as high as the ones back home but they are real, they exist. The public buildings are solid, occasionally impressive; they form walls against the menace of the all-but-empty space in which man's consequence is that of a handful of dust. The buildings can't shut out the sky, of course, but they impose limits on it.

If, however, you feel at home in the middle of vast empty spaces – and some people like myself do – you will resent Regina. And every other prairie city. They are alien eruptions on the face of nature, they disturb the harmony of a world in which the steel-and-glass ant-hills of modern man are an impertinence.

The massive, domed Provincial Legislative Building – which looks exactly like dozens of other massive domed legislative buildings scattered over the continent – stands fronting an artificial lake. The lake is an always muddy and sometimes ill-smelling triumph of the human spirit; to create a body of water of any kind in Regina is an authentic miracle.

There are some things in Regina worth seeing. The splendid Museum of Natural History, one of the finest of its kind on the continent, is quite properly a source of civic and provincial pride; and the R.C.M.P. barracks, the western training centre for recruits to the Force, draws thousands of visitors during the summer months. An interesting museum is open to the public, and red-coated Mounties are always on exhibit during visiting hours.

For nine months of the year the citizens of Regina are a sober, well-ordered folk not much given to emotional display. The stranger will find little evidence among them of the back-slapping exuberance alleged to be characteristic of the native Westerner. Their attitude towards sports is one of indifference; baseball they reject out of hand, hockey they barely tolerate. But in August a queer kind of madness falls upon the city; every other Saturday afternoon from early fall till late November – be it hot or cold or moist or dry – these same sober citizens and their fellows from as far away as Saskatoon and Prince Albert jam Taylor Field Stadium to urge on in a Bacchic frenzy the imported tanks on legs who are the

Saskatchewan Roughriders football team. Regina's passion for football is beyond the comprehension of the ordinary mortal. It needs
a sociologist to explain it and a prairie Pindar to celebrate it.

Between Regina and Moose Jaw no islands of scrubby bush dot
the surface of the immense sea of land – the great plains stretch
uninterrupted to the perimeter of the horizon. This is the authentic
wheat country, the original bread-basket of the world. The rich
gumbo soil is an adhesive nightmare when wet but it produces the
world's finest wheat – Number One Hard.

Moose Jaw squats in a tangle of ravines and valleys at the con-
fluence of the Thunder and Moose Jaw creeks. The immensely
wide main street is lined with substantial, reticent, old-world buildings – the visitor from abroad subconsciously looks for a Lyons
Corner House and a Barclay's Bank at every intersection. But the
stolid, dignified appearance of the city is at odds with its reputation
– in the roaring twenties Moose Jaw roared louder than any other
town in the West. River Street was an internationally celebrated
criminal hideout, half the city police force were arrested for various
misdemeanours, and the Ku Klux Klan – whose Saskatchewan
membership in the twenties is said to have numbered 40,000 –
made Moose Jaw the centre of its prairie activities and proclaimed
white supremacy and burned fiery crosses in a cow-pasture adjacent
to the city. Some residents insist that the spirit of the twenties isn't
altogether dead, that even today Moose Jaw is capable on occasion
of hiking up her ultra-respectable skirts to reveal the sequined G-
string of the ageing but still uninhibited queen of the honky-tonk.

Visitors interested in caged wildlife will no doubt enjoy the
animal park which encloses 500 acres along the Moose Jaw Creek.
But the enduring attraction of the city must always be its name.
Moose Jaw, Saskatchewan, is an irresistible combination; like
Medicine Hat and Walla Walla and Oshkosh, it lures from distant
places seekers after the exotic, the off-beat. (My wife and I once
made a detour of several hundred miles through rugged Wyoming
mountain country for no other reason than to see what two towns
named Spotted Horse and Ten Sleep looked like. Except for the

bars, they looked exactly like any two Saskatchewan towns of comparable size.)

The name is said to be a creation of an Indian who observed a white man on the bank of the creek mending his broken cart with the jaw of a moose—a feat of improvisation well worth the Indian's attention. The story — to be regarded with the utmost respect and dubiety—was probably the creation of a publicity genius living in advance of his time.

West of Moose Jaw the Highway is bordered at frequent intervals by alkali sloughs. When the stagnant malodorous water evaporates it leaves a filmy white deposit which whips up in smoke-like clouds — sometimes deceiving the stranger into thinking he is running into a prairie fire — and dances in weird devil's jigs across the Highway. At Chaplin fifty miles west of Moose Jaw a sodium sulphate plant, one of several scattered throughout the province, squats in a dismal swamp of hell and converts the alkali deposits to commercial uses.

Swift Current, a hundred miles west of Moose Jaw, is a neon-bedecked oasis in a valley of dry bones, a pleasant stopping-place if the time is right. Swift Current is renowned in the West for its Dominion Experimental Station (the second-largest in Canada) and its boom-or-bust extravagances. Traditionally its citizens are either driving late-model Cadillacs or flat broke.

In 1885, the year of the Riel Rebellion, a force of Canadian militia detrained at Swift Current, then a huddle of shacks at the end of steel, and marched north to the relief of Battleford, for several weeks harassed by bands of Indians more intent on plunder than scalps. The militia under the command of Colonel Otter made the 150-mile march in five days, chased away the Indians, and were heroes for an hour. Unfortunately, and for no justifiable reason, Otter led his green youngsters into the Eagle Hills to punish Chief Poundmaker for failing to control his braves. The militia were badly defeated at Cutknife Hill and ironically escaped complete disaster only by courtesy of Poundmaker who kept his exuberant warriors under the strictest control and refused to allow them to pursue the retreating enemy.

The Highway continues its course along a desolate valley-floor.

The general pattern of landscape is unchanged; grain elevators still loom against the skyline and the next town is always in sight. But imperceptibly the valley widens, loses its outline; the road curves, rises, falls – and by-passes a town with the unlikely name of Piapot, so-called in honour of a Piegan chief who attempted to hold up the progress of the C.P.R. (which he quite properly distrusted) by camping on the right-of-way. Inevitably he and his braves were removed without bloodshed by the ubiquitous Mounties – two of them.

To the traveller weary of elevators and grain-fields and the black ribbon snaking its way forever around low buttes and over sun-burnt ridges, the attraction of the land now lies to the south. Incredibly, a range of hills has come into view. They hang blue and remote between heaven and earth – but they are unmistakably real.

The Cypress Hills, occupying an area of over a thousand square miles, lie a few miles north of Montana and astride the Saskatchewan-Alberta border. They rise to a height of nearly 5,000 feet and form the highest point of land in Canada between Labrador and the Rockies. An island in the last ice-age – so some geologists theorize – the Hills constitute an unglaciated area which has preserved its own peculiar growths; there survive in the hills species of fauna and flora found nowhere else in Canada (many of them indigenous to regions hundreds of miles farther south). They include such exotic and alarming specimens of wildlife as solpugids (a species of scorpion), hog-nosed vipers, kangaroo rats, and black-widow spiders. Fortunately these are all retiring creatures that live far off the beaten path in those parts of the hills and surrounding sun-baked terrain where yucca grass, prickly-pear cactus, and sage-brush flourish.

The Cypress Hills divide the American High Plains from that vast area of plain and forest and tundra once known as Prince Rupert's Land. There are points among the hills where it is possible for a man to stand and see streams flowing in opposite directions, to trace in the mind's eye the course of the south-bound water into the great Missouri-Mississippi system via the Milk River and on into the steaming Gulf of Mexico – or follow the north-bound streams across the great plains and into the Saskatchewan River basin to empty at last into the mist-haunted chill arctic indentation of Hudson Bay. Waters that have a common source end their journeyings five thousand miles apart – the Cypress Hills are quite literally the top of a continent.

In the days before the coming of the white man, the Cypress Hills country was a natural game sanctuary, and neutral ground between the Indian tribes who circled around the base of the hills and frequently penetrated them but never took permanent possession: the Cree and powerful Blackfoot Confederacy to the north and west, the Assiniboine, Crow, Nez Percé, and Sioux to the east and south. Palliser was the first white man to report on the hills – 'a perfect oasis in the desert we have travelled'. Métis moving out of Red River following the disturbances of 1870-1 found a pastoral paradise among the hills, although the majority of those who made the trek west preferred to settle several hundred miles farther north. The Hudson's Bay Company established a post in the hills in 1871 but abandoned it the following year, leaving the fur trade to the independents from across the border who, unlike the Great Company, were happy to swap whisky for furs. The massacre of a large band of Assiniboine Indians by drunken traders in 1873 hastened the formation of the North West Mounted Police; and three years later the red-coats built Fort Walsh in the heart of the hills. The law had come to stay.

No tourist, however rushed, should miss spending at least a day among the hills, for they encompass within their modest limits more history, more authentic folklore, and more unique charm than any comparable area in the West. Maple Creek, a sleepy, rather un-Western-looking town – the public buildings are brick, the houses old, the streets pleasantly shaded – is the turning-off place for the hills. The highway south (No. 21) rises steadily over a stretch of twenty miles to a height of 4,000 feet and a point where a rustic gate invites entry into the Cypress Hills Provincial Park.

My family and I first visited the park many years ago, and the memory of that experience still lingers like a gracious benediction – a memory of the rich, rank smells of evergreen and woodsmoke and bacon frying over a pot-bellied stove in an unvarnished old log

Lake among the Cypress Hills

hut; of the sight of water fringed on all sides by tall lodge-pine (a miracle in south-western Saskatchewan); and of a sunset view over half Saskatchewan from an eminence prosaically called Bald Butte, a view so softened, magical in the half-light – all harsh geometric lines subdued, blatant colours modified – as to suggest that Bald Butte must have been the point from which the devil tempted Christ with a view of all the kingdoms of the earth. The memory of that first evening has drawn us back to the hills summer after summer; they are to us the best-known, best-loved region of the West.

The park facilities are unimpressive and the tiny lake around which they cluster isn't much good for swimming or fishing. But the hills themselves are what matter. Perhaps the most exciting short drive in Saskatchewan is the one leading south-west from the park over a winding dirt road for twenty odd miles to Fort Walsh. Herds of white-faces dot the slopes as far as the eye can see, grazing knee-deep in the lush grass of the wide valley-bottoms (the hills average four inches more of moisture per year than the surrounding plains), and as likely as not a herd of antelope will come into view on a far-off ridge. The road snakes its way across hills and ravines and through a ranchman's yard, winds up a precipitous slope to a high plateau, then plunges down the other side into the valley of the Battle Creek.

Fort Walsh, named in honour of one of the first commissioners of the North West Mounted Police, was built in the valley of the Battle in 1876. None too soon, for 1876 was a bad year in the hills. The great buffalo herds had all but vanished from the surrounding plains, and hunger drove the Indians into the hills where a few herds still survived. Here the red man made his last stand in the West for the way of life he knew and loved; here on the neutral ground lived uneasily the tribes from the adjacent Canadian plains, side by side with hordes of sullen, restless refugees from across the American border. Here in 1876 came Sitting Bull and his fierce Sioux warriors, fresh from their triumph over the cream of the U.S. cavalry at the Battle of the Little Big Horn; and here a handful of men in red coats fed the hungry, proclaimed the Queen's law, and compelled white man and Indian alike to accept it.

Old Fort Walsh has long since disappeared. The fort standing in the valley today is not a restoration but a reconstruction. The barracks, stables, guard-room, kitchens, palisades are built to scale and no doubt provide an accurate visual picture of the original. But the spirit of the past lingers uneasily if at all among these shiny, painted replicas; its true dwelling-place is the abiding hills, and the little graveyard a few hundred yards from Fort Walsh, on the rim of the great valley.

In the graveyard lie the bodies of a dozen or more of the men of the North West Mounted Police. What is significant about the inscriptions engraved on the modest headstones is this: only one records death by violence. Constable Marmaduke Graeburn, aged nineteen, was murdered; the others in the graveyard died prosaically of pneumonia and dysentery and typhoid. Indirectly these inscriptions constitute the highest tribute that can be paid to the men who in 1876 went into the hills, for they make it clear that they went not to fight the Indians but to save them.

The peaceful settlement of the Canadian West by contrast with the violence which marked the opening of the American frontier stemmed in part from the foresight of the Dominion government in placing a force of policemen on the prairies well in advance of the main tide of settlers. On the American frontier army forces arrived long after savage warfare between white man and Indian had become part of the frontier pattern; and many of the army men, veterans of four years' atrocious civil conflict, assumed that the simplest way to establish peace was to kill all the Indians. But much of the credit for the peaceful settlement of the Canadian West must go to the men of the original police force. Their courage and endurance were beyond question; and most of the members, particularly those with Old Country backgrounds, assumed almost by instinct the role of guardians over lesser breeds without the law. Lieutenant William Butler, the British Army officer who accompanied Colonel Wolseley to Winnipeg and afterwards investigated conditions prevailing among the Plains Indians and traders, reported in 1871 that a force of not more than 150 men was needed to maintain order throughout the territory reaching from the eastern Manitoba border to the Rockies. Butler had seen service in many outposts of empire including India, and his faith in the power and integrity of men doing the work of empire touches either the ridiculous or the sublime — perhaps a little of both. That faith was shared by the members of the Force and countless times it carried them triumphantly and without bloodshed through situations which seemed certain to end in fighting and death. They were the kind of men from whose exploits great legends spring. In a time when it has become fashionable to denigrate the achievements of the old North West Mounted Police we would do well to remember that legends contain the essence of truth.

In the long run, the Mounties failed to save the Indian, but only because not even men in red coats could reverse the immutable course of history.

The obvious way to leave Saskatchewan and enter Alberta is by the Highway through the border town of Walsh a few miles west of Maple Creek. But those travellers who long for a few hours' escape from gas fumes and asphalt and high speeds should do as my wife and I did on our trans-Canada journey — make the crossing by way of the winding municipal roads and rutted private trails that haphazardly link the Cypress Hills Provincial Park on the Saskatchewan side with Elkwater Park in Alberta, twenty-five miles south of the Highway and forty-odd miles from Medicine Hat. It is a route — unofficial, mostly unmarked — that takes you past Fort Walsh and out of the valley of the Battle up on to high, bare ridges from which immense vistas open up both north and south, bringing into view on a clear day the Bearpaw Mountains in Montana. It gives you a chance, too, to meet authentic ranchers and cow-pokes, for you are sure to get lost several times and will have to ask your way. ('Just take that trail over the hill,' one weather-beaten cow-hand told us. 'She'll drop you down the other side into so-and-so's back yard.' She did, too. Literally – our faithful car leaning back like a well-trained mustang and digging in her heels all the way down.)

Some day, no doubt, an excellent paved road impossible to stray from will link the two parks; but for a few years longer the crazy trails snaking among the rounded hills and over the great ridges will enable us to slip back into a world which – except for the occasional jet streaking across the heavens – differs hardly at all from the one Lieutenant William Butler saw nearly a century ago and described, better than anyone before or since, in his classic of western travel, *The Great Lone Land*:

'The great ocean itself does not present more infinite variety than does this prairie-ocean of which we speak. In winter, a dazzling surface of purest snow; in early summer, a vast expanse of grass and pale pink roses; in autumn too often a wild sea of raging fire. No ocean of water in the world can vie with its gorgeous sunsets; no solitude can equal the loneliness of a night-shadowed prairie; one feels the stillness and hears the silence, the wail of the prowling wolf makes the voice of solitude audible, the stars look down through infinite silence on a silence almost as intense. . . . But for my part, the prairies had nothing terrible in their aspect, nothing oppressive in their loneliness. One saw here the world as it had taken shape and form from the hands of the Creator. Nor did the scene look less beautiful because nature alone tilled the earth, and the unaided sun brought forth the flowers.'

ALBERTA

Medicine Hat is a name and a story. It is a few other things besides. It is the first important town on the Trans-Canada Highway inside the Alberta border; and – although unfortunately identified in the public mind with a plethora of publicity-conscious rain-makers, flag-pole sitters, and extrovert mayors – a pleasant place to live in and pleasing to the eye. Sprawled along the flats and banks of the South Saskatchewan River in the middle of a vast semi-arid region given over mainly to ranching, Medicine Hat is a cow-town in spirit and in fact, and an industrial centre of some importance because of its unlimited supply of natural gas. But the name and the story are what matter.

A dozen legends, none altogether convincing, explain the name. The saving of the name is the story.

In 1907 Rudyard Kipling, then at the height of his fame (he had just won the Nobel Prize), stopped off in Medicine Hat while on a trans-Canada tour. The members of the Cypress Club, mostly old-timers of assorted occupations and political views, took Kipling in hand and saved him from the horrors of an orthodox civic reception. 'We just met him as man to man, in all our rustic habits,' a member of the club reported. 'We talked to him as if he was a beef-buyer and really had a whale of a time. Of course R.K. ate it up and hated to tear himself away.' The great man showed his immediate appreciation of the club's hospitality by coining a catch-phrase used ever since to describe Medicine Hat – 'the city with all hell for a basement'. But the really grand gesture was yet to come.

Three years after Kipling's visit, Medicine Hat experienced the building-and-real-estate boom inevitable in a Western town near the beginning of the century. The boom lasted just long enough to flood the town with dull-spirited, ignorant new-comers who denounced its name as an embarrassing absurdity and demanded that it be changed forthwith to something respectable, something 'that has a sound like the name of a man's best girl and looks like business at the head of a financial report' – to quote the Calgary *Herald*, which had no business butting in. The city council, conventional hustling business types to a man, ordered a plebiscite to settle the issue. Those stout upholders of the ancient ways, the members of the Cypress Club, knowing the outcome of the plebiscite to be a foregone conclusion and the triumph of respectability over tradition inevitable, were morose and disconsolate men until at a wake in the club-rooms a member, whose name unfortunately has been lost in the mists of time, raised from his beer-mug a face suddenly illumined with a deep and holy joy and said, 'Kipling should know of this – he'd flay the hide off those blighters.'

The thought was instantly translated into action. The club member delegated to write to Kipling was the local postmaster, Frank Fatt. An excellent choice, for Mr. Fatt was no mean hand with a pen. His letter is an eloquent plea to 'the Father Confessor of the Empire' to save the name of the town on behalf of the old-timers. 'Here we have courted our sweethearts, married and begot children and built our homes, driving our tent pegs deep into Mother Earth,' Mr. Fatt cried out in impassioned accents, 'and here we remain to hold up the old British tradition as long as the good God gives us breath.'

Mr. Fatt's plea is not, however, entirely sentimental rhapsody – he reveals a pretty talent himself for flaying the hides off the new-comers, 'the sons of Belial who have arisen and want to change the name of the city. It smacks too much of the Injun, smells fearfully of the tepee fire and kini-ki-nick, reminds outsiders of the whacking lies (may God forgive them) of the U.S. newspaper men in regard to our weather and so forth. In a moment of weakness our city fathers have decided to submit the question to the vote of the rate-payers instead of ordering the proposers to be cast into a den of fiery rattlesnakes.'

Then follows the appeal direct:

'Can you help us with a few words of encouragement in combating these heretics? Your influence here is great. If it is shown that you are against this proposition, it will help us materially.'

Kipling obliged. His letter to Mr. Fatt, dated from Bateman's Burwash, Sussex, is a devastating combination of sentiment, logic, and invective. It deserves to be quoted at length:

'... You tell me that a public vote is to be taken on the question of changing the city's name. So far as I can make out ... the chief arguments for the change are (a) that some U.S. journalists have some sort of joke that Medicine Hat supplies all the bad weather of the U.S. and (b) that another name would look better at the head of a prospectus. ...

'Now as to the charge of brewing bad weather, etc., I see no reason on earth why white men should be fluffed out of their city's birthright by an imported joke. Accept the charge joyously and proudly and go forward as Medicine Hat – the only city officially recognized as capable of freezing out the United States and giving the continent cold feet. ...

'To my mind the name of Medicine Hat ... echoes as you so justly put it the old Cree and Blackfoot tradition of red mystery and romance that once filled the prairies. ... Believe me, the very name is an asset, and as years go on will become more and more of an asset. It has no duplicate in the world; it makes men ask questions ... draws the feet of young men towards it; it has the qualities of uniqueness, individuality, assertion, and power. Above all, it is the lawful, original, sweat-and-dust-won name of the city, and to change it would be to risk the luck of the city, to disgust and dishearten old-timers, not in the city alone, but the world over, and to advertise abroad the city's lack of faith in itself. Men do not think much of a family which has risen in the world, changing its name for social reasons. They think still less of a man who because he is successful repudiates the wife who stood by him in his early struggles. I do not know what I should say, but I have the clearest notion of what I should think of a town that went back on itself. ...

'In conclusion, it strikes me that the two arguments put forward for the change of the name are almost equally bad. The second is perhaps a shade worse than the first. In the first case the town would change its name in the hope of making more money under an alias or, as the Calgary *Herald* writes, for the sake of a name that "has a sound like the name of a man's best girl and looks like business at the head of a financial report".

'But a man's city is a trifle more than a man's best girl. She is the living background of his life and love and toil and hope and sorrow and joy. Her success is his success; her shame is his shame; her honour is his honour; and her good name is his good name.

'What, then, should a city be rechristened that has sold its name? Judasville.'

The members of the Cypress Club saw to it that Kipling's letter was given nation-wide publicity and the sons of Belial were silenced. They have remained silent ever since.

Recently Mr. E. J. Goodwin, editor of the Medicine Hat *News*, performed a fine public service when he compiled a pamphlet, free to anyone dropping into the *News* office, containing the complete Fatt-Kipling correspondence.

Medicine Hat is near the centre of the Canadian short-grass country – the third Prairie Steppe – a lonely, desolate plain furrowed by dry, eroded coulees where nothing grows except tufted short-grass and sagebrush and greasewood and prickly-pear cactus. Attempts to dry-farm the short-grass country have drawn bitter comments from the cattlemen who just naturally hate farmers anyway – 'Ain't it a shame how them damn weasels has tore up all the country north of the Bow? She's so bloody gravelly underneath she won't grow grass for a goose, and them simple bastards expect to grow wheat!' So far the attempts appear largely unsuccessful. There are stretches of the Highway between Medicine Hat and Brooks, seventy miles farther north-west, where literally nothing breaks the monotony of the

Alberta

prairie land except the Highway and the telephone line. Not a tree, house, or living creature disturbs the surface of a plain rolling to the most distant horizon the eye ever strained to reach. It is while driving over such stretches that individuals of a gregarious nature develop an intense affection for a strip of asphalt. The Highway becomes a symbol of humanity in a land virtually devoid of all other suggestion of life.

There are places on the earth that assume immense importance not because of *what* they are but *where*. Brooks, Alberta, is one of these places. It is the centre of an irrigation district, the site of a horticultural experimental station, a town of tree-lined streets and lush green lawns in the middle of a treeless, barren desolation. But anyone wishing to see the epitome of man's determination to make the desert rejoice and blossom like the rose should leave the town and drive south ten miles to Lake Newall and Kinbrook Park.

Kinbrook Park is an artificial island rising from an artificial lake and studded with thousands of hand-planted trees. Lake Newall is a great reservoir covering forty square miles, created by pouring water from the dammed-up Bow River into a depression on the prairie; the island is a ridge of land surmounting the surrounding depression.

Judged by the standards prevailing in moister parts of the earth, Kinbrook Park is no beauty spot. The trees are mostly small and scraggly, the surrounding landscape featureless, the cottages huddled along the lakeshore a gaudy-hued offence to aesthetic sensibilities (several of them are painted a curious piebald, no doubt a reflection of cow-country influence). No beauty spot, but a genuine phenomenon: The lake is clear and deep, the artificially created sand beaches of generous expanse, the picnic- and camp-site facilities excellent. Fishing is an advertised attraction, but after a conversation in the park with a man from North Dakota I hesitate to recommend it.

The man from North Dakota was drunk. Very drunk. At five in the afternoon. 'Got the flu,' he explained. 'Gives a man the shakes.' He stared at the lake with bloodshot eyes. 'Come up for the fishin',' he said after a while. 'Fishin's no goddam good.' 'Wrong time of year,' I suggested wisely, but the man from North Dakota paid me no heed. 'Been comin' here every year for thirteen year,' he said. 'Fishin's never any goddam good.'

I pondered. Why should a man come all the way from North Dakota for thirteen years straight to fish an artificial lake in the middle of an Alberta desert? No doubt *any* body of water would be a marvel to a man from North Dakota, but there were several a good deal nearer home. But I did not ask any questions for I had no wish to pry into the secret places of his soul. Every man, I suppose, pursues in his own peculiar fashion his own peculiar Grail.

Kinbrook Park is a man-made wonder. Thirty miles north-east of Brooks lies a natural wonder which the traveller who relishes the unexpected and spectacular should spend an hour or two exploring.

The gravelled municipal road to the Steveville Dinosaur Park cuts through irrigated farmlands past farmsteads all of which look alike. Gorgeously coloured pheasants stroll across the road introducing a touch of the exotic, the bizarre, into an otherwise prosaic, neatly patterned world of squares, rectangles, and identical windbreaks. Brooks is the centre of a famous pheasant hatchery, and every fall, hunters, many of them from the United States, swarm into the district for the annual pheasant slaughter which no doubt is excellent for business.

Like so many natural phenomena of the prairies, the badlands of the Red Deer River burst upon you without the slightest warning. Steveville Dinosaur Park is a Dantesque nightmare, a wild eerie region of eroded hoodoos, fantastically distorted monstrous shapes of earth rising from the valley-floor between towering canyon walls. Along the valley-floor the Red Deer River runs sluggishly past dismal sagebrush flats, and the stunted trees lining its banks have been twisted by wind and flood into grotesque witch-figures fit to haunt a man's sleep if seen by moonlight.

The badlands of the Red Deer are an authentic valley of dry bones. Most of the region has been well picked over in the past thirty or forty years, but anyone with enough enthusiasm and energy to dig in an out-of-the-way spot may be lucky enough to make a bone-strike. Several skeletons of prehistoric monsters are on exhibit within the park, including the fenced-in remains of a 'Duckbill Dinosaur, *laying* just as found' (italics mine).

No doubt for most visitors the attraction of the Steveville Dinosaur Park palls after an hour or two because the region is so completely devoid of human associations. The Indians avoided it like the

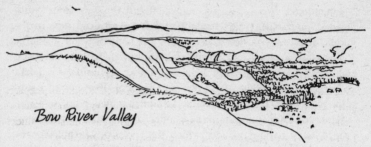

Bow River Valley

plague, and the Canadian West never nurtured the kind of bad man
who might have been driven to seek refuge there. Similar regions in
Montana and Wyoming have resounded to the thunder of hooves
and the crack of Winchesters and the whirring of movie-cameras,
but the only sound to disturb the silence of the Red Deer badlands
for ages past has been the clank of the excavator's shovel. The entire
valley from Steveville to Drumheller, a hundred miles north-west, is
one vast prehistoric graveyard.

A few miles west of Brooks the contour of the land changes — or
perhaps it would be more accurate to say it acquires contours. The
Bow River valley dominates the landscape, rising in precipitous
bluffs and vast rolling swells to relieve the monotony of the great
plain. Four miles off the Highway and three miles south of the
village of Cluny is a spot splendid to look at, rich in history — the
very heart of the Blackfoot country. Only a man insensitive to beauty
and with no concern for the romance and heartbreak of time past
can look down the long valley-slope to the old Blackfoot Crossing
and remain unmoved.

Here from time immemorial the Indians of the Blackfoot Confederacy crossed the Bow River on their endless north-south journeyings; here they rendezvoused, pitched their tents, plotted war
against their ancient enemies the Crees, and sometimes smoked the
pipe of peace. And here in the year 1877 on the south bank of the
river they signed away their heritage, the land of their ancestors.

On a high bluff overlooking the Crossing a cairn commemorates
the signing of Blackfoot Treaty Number Seven. On that day in
1877, 4,000 Indians of the Blackfoot Confederacy — Blackfoot,

Blood, Stony, Piegan, Sarcee – pitched their tents at the Crossing, and there the great Chief Crowfoot and his fellows met in solemn council with the commissioners of the Great White Queen. Nearly a hundred members of the North West Mounted Police added to the pomp and pageantry of a ceremony which marked the end of a long day's dying – the day of the red man. Crowfoot and his people, in return for a few scattered reserves and five dollars a year of treaty money, surrendered to the Queen, 'for as long as the sun shines and rivers run', the land which is now south-western Alberta.

Romantic souls who share Cyrano de Bergerac's view that 'one does not fight because there is hope of winning – it is much finer to fight when it is no use' may feel that Crowfoot would have done better to lead his people, like Sitting Bull and Chief Joseph of the Nez Percé, in one last desperate campaign against the white intruder, rather than submit tamely to his demands. Had he done so the history of the Canadian West would have been more colourful because bloodier. But Crowfoot was not a romantic, he was a realist who accepted the inevitable. By 1877 the buffalo had all but disappeared from the prairie and with their going the old way of life went too. Crowfoot was no lover of the white man but he saw in him the only hope of salvation for his people. And having pledged his word he kept it. When, eight years after the signing of the treaty, the Métis under Louis Riel set the West aflame, Crowfoot refused to give ear to Riel's emissaries and held his restless, disillusioned braves in check. The Council of the Northwest Territories rewarded Crowfoot for his loyalty with a gift of fifty dollars and the C.P.R. gave him a lifetime pass that he hardly ever used.

Perhaps had Crowfoot foreseen the fate of his people he would have gone down fighting.

Crowfoot lived out his last years on the Blackfoot reservation near the Crossing. A memorial plaque on the valley's rim marks the spot to which the great chief, feeling death upon him, was carried to look for the last time on the valley and the Crossing. (Just as another aristocrat, Sir Walter Scott – who would have admired Crowfoot – paused on his last sad journey to Abbotsford to bid farewell to his beloved Tweed.) Crowfoot must have yielded reluctantly to death, knowing that he would find no fairer land in any Happy

Hunting Ground. The valley swells in great folds to meet the immensity of over-arching sky, and the river snakes along the valley-floor, flowing from the far-off mountains that serrate the western skyline – white wave-crests frozen into eternal stillness. A great land to live in. A land hard to leave.

Crowfoot is buried in the Indian graveyard that overlooks the Crossing from a high bluff. The graveyard is an austere and melancholy spot. Most of the graves are unmarked, but one massive slab to the memory of James Drunken Cheif (*sic*) stirs at least casual curiosity. A stone cairn inscribed with the meaningless phrase 'Father of his People' commemorates Crowfoot.

There are one or two other Crowfoot memorials in the vicinity of the Crossing, including a dingy railway whistle-stop (two grain elevators and a station-house) and a muddy creek. Thirty miles east, the attractive irrigation town of Bassano commemorates the name of an Italian nobleman, and it is just possible that the contrast between the Crowfoot and Bassano memorials may give rise to some interesting reflections on our sense of values. Crowfoot was merely the last great chief of a once-great people, but the Marquis de Bassano held shares in the C.P.R.

The Highway side-swipes Calgary along her northern flank and it is easy to by-pass the city. Few of us are likely to do so, for Calgary is one of the two glamour cities of Canada. (The other is, of course, Montreal.) Her history is prosaic – a record of steady, sometimes spectacular growth from Mounted Police fort (1875) to cow-town to oil-town. But the great Calgary Stampede, Canada's most celebrated annual show, has given the city nearly world-wide publicity. The white Stetson hat has become her symbol, cow-town her *nom de plume*. Even the athletic teams that represent the city are invariably Broncos or Stampeders and they play hockey in the Corral. To the hundreds of thousands of visitors who throng the Stampede grounds and the thousands of passing tourists who don't stay long enough to learn the truth, Calgary epitomizes the spirit and tradition of the old West.

Calgary enjoys what is perhaps the finest scenic location of all our cities – only Quebec, Montreal, and Vancouver can offer serious competition. The Bow and Elbow rivers form a junction near her heart, the foothills roll away in great hump-backed swells on three sides, and on the fourth the wide valley of the Bow reaches back to the mountains sixty miles west, and the mountains, abrupt, massive, snow-capped, form a stunning back-drop against the wide sky.

The city itself is unworthy of its setting. Architecturally Calgary is a stereotype of the typical modern big town. Office skyscrapers no more or less imaginative than the general run dominate the city's centre, and the fungus-like growths of suburbia blotch the fair face of the Bow River valley and surrounding hill-sides. Unlike such western United States cities as Denver and Salt Lake City, Calgary takes no colour from her surroundings – she is Regina or Moose Jaw or Lethbridge cast in a larger mould. She sits at the very heart of a great range country, but a cowboy is seldom seen on her main streets, and when he does appear he is an anachronism. His true Saturday-night home of the spirit is the small, authentic cow-town like Medicine Hat or Maple Creek.

The truth is that Calgary is not a cow-town any more but a booming oil-town and one of Canada's important financial centres. Making money is Calgary's real business. The Turner Valley oil strike of 1913 laid the foundation of the modern city's prosperity and determined her view and way of life. Oil in the immediate vicinity has long since petered out but most of the great oil companies and scores of smaller ones maintain their western headquarters in Calgary. The man in the white Stetson hat, cowboy boots, and Cadillac is nine times out of ten an oil tycoon.

Apart from making money, the favourite pastime of Calgarians is feuding with Edmonton, the capital city of the province. Calgary has never forgiven Edmonton for being both provincial capital and the site of the provincial university. (Things were much better arranged in Saskatchewan – Regina got the Legislature, Saskatoon the University; as a result inter-city squabbling has been generally spasmodic and amicable.) But the feuding between the Alberta cities is sustained and seldom good-humoured. On the Calgary side, at least, it is now carried on in a spirit which reflects an odd combination of mature satiric wit and adolescent pique – a spirit admirably illustrated by an editorial in a Calgary paper attacking

Edmonton's admittedly absurd effort to jazz up its 1963 Exhibition by introducing a Klondike Days motif:

' . . . This is casting about for identity with a vengeance. In the field of capitalizing on someone else's glamorous past, this probably will forever stand as a world record.

'By what kind of yardstick, by what devious reasoning, can Edmonton be linked with the Klondike and its gold? . . .

'We're tempted to ask, when you think of Edmonton, what do you think of? Instead, we will state flatly that when you think of Edmonton, gold you most certainly do not think of.

'Snowdrifts, maybe, or iceworms. But not gold, by any stretch of the imagination. . . .

'It was possible to sympathize with Edmonton's search for a soul. But in attempting to emulate Calgary (which wisely chose to glorify its authentic heritage), Edmonton has emerged as a city of desperation.

'Even Calgary could stage a Klondike Days with a truer ring. At least the citizens here enjoy a certain affluence.

'Why doesn't Edmonton just put up a booth at the Calgary Stampede and forget about trying to do something on its own?'

Calgary's decision to 'glorify its authentic heritage' has been a money-making proposition. But let no innocent visitor to the Stampede be deceived into thinking that he is watching the true sons of the Canadian West in action. The star performers before the grandstand – except the chuckwagon drivers – are nearly all hard-bitten professional entertainers who follow the great summer rodeo circuit over half the continent, ending up in Madison Square Garden. Local small-town rodeos, and there are many of them, lack the glamour and the hysterical excitement of the Second Greatest Show on Earth, but they are in many ways more rewarding for they reflect to a far greater degree the authentic spirit of the range country.

Calgary is a bright, airy, obvious town, all her wares on display, no unexpected delights hidden around corners. Although she boasts a university, a symphony orchestra, a fine arts centre, and numerous other adjuncts of conventional culture, it is safe to say that Calgary has no wish to be the Athens of the West. She would much sooner be the Houston.

But let not her frailties be remembered. Calgary women are among the most beautiful in Canada and, outside Montreal, the best dressed.

Calgary caters admirably to tourists. Other cities are content to settle for a motel strip – Calgary, characteristically, boasts a motel village. It is conveniently located at the junction of the Trans-Canada Highway and No. 1A; and there, except during Stampede Week, the tourist is almost certain to find adequate accommodation.

Driving the Highway from Calgary into the mountains can be a dangerous experience. The Highway itself is new, superbly engineered, adequately posted – the hazards are scenic rather than technical. The temptations to take your eye from the road ahead are frequent and almost irresistible, but resisted they must be, for the flow of traffic is sure to be heavy. Tourists swarm across the border into southern Alberta and up the Fort Macleod–Calgary Trail to join the hordes from the East already pounding towards the mountains at seventy miles an hour. Unfortunately – and this is the only possible criticism of the Trans-Canada Highway between Calgary and Banff – look-outs are few, and the man behind the wheel must be content to observe in disconnected snatches the stupendous wall of mountain ahead.

On the Calgary-Banff run the Highway passes through splendidly uncluttered country, much of it an Indian reserve. Thirty miles out of Calgary a side-road leads across the Bow River to the Stony Indian settlement of Morley, and the little church built by the missionaries George MacDougall and his son John in 1872. The church, unused since 1921, has recently been restored and stands out bravely in its new coat of white and green paint on the bare north bank of the rushing Bow. The tourist pavilion that has been built immediately adjacent to the church may appear an incongruity unless we can bring ourselves to regard it as an up-to-date parish hall.

Four years after building the church the Rev. George MacDougall died in a blizzard at a spot a few miles north of the church-site.

MacDougall's church stands beside the old Banff highway, now numbered 1A, and familiarly called the Banff Trail. In some respects the old highway is even more scenic than the new – at certain points it affords a broader panorama embracing the entire sweep of the Bow Valley and the mountains beyond. One of the finest views in all Canada is that from the turn-out at the top of the great hill above the village of Cochrane twenty miles west of Calgary – a magnificent expanse of river, valley, foothills, mountains, and over-arching sky juxtaposed in a flawlessly balanced harmony, so flawless as to suggest a deliberately contrived artistic improvement on nature. It is a view of which no man can ever tire, for although the elements are fixed, permanent, the colour- and cloud-patterns change minute by minute so that the communicated effect is of something at once enduring and at the same time forever new.

The forestry road into the Kananaskis Forest Reserve lying south of the Highway provides another admirable diversion for the adventurous traveller. The turn-off, marked by a garage, a store, and a modest sign, is easy to miss. The gravelled road runs a total of 139 miles south to the town of Coleman in the Crowsnest Pass, but for the Trans-Canada traveller a side-trip to the nearest camp-site – about twenty miles – will be enough to assure him that the relatively unpublicized Kananaskis Forest Reserve is one of the most magnificent and least cluttered mountain and lake regions in all Canada. The mountains west of the road rise to a height of over 11,000 feet – higher than at Banff. The road is sometimes rough in spots but always safe; and driving over it for even a few miles satisfies the urge in all of us to do something a little different, off-beat – permits us to cherish a secret delight knowing that nearly everyone else is tearing straight on for Banff.

The plainsman like myself is likely to find his first plunge into the mountains on the Calgary-Banff run an alarming experience. Not because of the Highway gradients, which are gentle, nor the curves, which are also gentle and well-banked, but because of the sudden feeling of being separated from all familiar things. Before we are aware of what is happening the beautiful but sinister Three Sisters and assorted kinfolk have slipped in behind us and cut off our retreat. But the valley ahead broadens – there is still room to breathe. We are not yet fenced in. Not quite.

Canmore is the only town between Calgary and Banff. Once a flourishing mining community, it now survives by means invisible to mortal sight. The ardent student of Canadiana should, however, slip off the Highway long enough to look at Canmore's modest United Church. A missionary named Charles Gordon was its builder and first minister; tradition alleges that young Gordon, better known to the world as Ralph Connor, wrote his first novel, *Black Rock: a Tale of the Selkirks*, in the study of the little church. The tradition is inaccurate – *Black Rock* was written in Winnipeg – but the basic material of the novel and several others including *The Sky Pilot* and *The Prospector* stems from the young missionary's experiences during the four years he was in charge of the Banff pastorate, a district covering 20,000 square miles of mountain and foothill.

No doubt the present generation knows not Joseph, but Ralph Connor deserves to be remembered in a money-conscious age if only because he was the first and almost only Canadian to make a small fortune from his books. *Black Rock* alone, originally intended as a series of sketches describing life in a western mining town and re-shaped into the semblance of a novel, sold over 300,000 copies.

The Canmore United – originally Presbyterian – Church, built under the direction of Ralph Connor, is one more reminder – there are many throughout the West – of the influence of the missionaries on the development of Western Canada from the early days of the nineteenth century. Robert Rundle carried the Word to the Blackfoot of the Banff district as early as 1840 – his memorial is the grand mountain towering over the valley of the Bow a few miles east of Banff. The MacDougalls, Father Lacombe, and a dozen other stouthearted champions of the Cross roamed the plains and mountain

valleys, founded their missions, fought the whisky-traders, and saved from destruction many Indian bodies and perhaps a few souls. In the restored frontier towns of the western United States the saloons, honky-tonks, and Boot Hills predominate, in western Canada the mission churches and Mounted Police posts. Strong men of God worked hand in hand with the Mounties to make the Canadian West a tough place for sinners.

It still is.

Most of us travelling the Trans-Canada Highway on holiday have certain objectives firmly rooted in the conscious or subconscious mind. Of these objectives Banff is certainly the most obvious and popular. It is the oldest, the best-known, and the best-loved national park in Canada.

Even the most jaded sophisticate must acknowledge that Banff is one of the loveliest spots on earth. Indeed, looking at the town and its environs from the summit of Sulphur Mountain you get the curious impression that in creating Banff, God assumed the role of a far-sighted parks superintendent and designed the area with a view to future tourism: planting a small, easily accessible mountain or two near the heart of things, a couple of larger ones – Rundle and Cascade – for scenic purposes at opposite ends of the town, directing a river, complete with picturesque falls yet suitable for boating, down a broad valley, studding the valley-floor and lower mountain-sides with magnificent evergreen forests (but leaving enough open space for a golf course), carving out a spectacular canyon or two within easy walking distance of the future town-site, banking the valley at both ends with solid mountain masses, and – the final touch of God-like benevolence – laying on an abundant supply of water, hot and cold.

Man has carried on the Creator's work with admirable discretion and good taste. The town of Banff appears characterless by design; and there is wisdom in such planning, for in such a setting the man-made could impose itself only through incongruity. The town buildings, both public and private, are unostentatious and so are the tourist accommodations. The many motels and hotels and private boarding-houses are comfortable – in a few instances luxurious – but all melt modestly into their environment, become a part of it. Even the neon lights seem subdued, their colours mostly soft pastels. The garish, the ornate, the ugly find no place in Banff.

With one exception. The Banff Springs Hotel sits overlooking the Bow Valley like a dowager duchess, an ageless relic of a bygone age casting an undimmed eye over the possessions she shares with no one – not even God. The hotel was almost completely rebuilt in 1928, but the remodellers worked in the spirit of an earlier and more grandiose time. Sir William Van Horne, who insisted that the original hotel be built in imitation of a French château to honour the early French fur-traders (few of whom had ever seen a château), would have approved the present design.

For those who can afford it – mostly Americans – the hotel provides all the amenities. But her chief value – impossible to think of a duchess as neuter – is as an act of defiance, a symbol of man's determination to impose something of himself, preserve his identity among the most awe-inspiring works of nature. Somerset Maugham has remarked that perfection is always a little dull; and perhaps the charm of the Banff Springs Hotel lies in her very incongruity – she adds the one essential touch of the freakish which prevents the perfection of Banff from becoming tiresome. For, whatever emotions she may arouse in those who contemplate her, boredom is certainly not one of them.

It is a tribute to those in charge of the park that even in the height of the tourist season Banff is a tranquil place. Night-life is almost non-existent – high altitudes and long walks (which can hardly be resisted) conspire to early and child-like slumber. The smell of evergreen overpowers the gas fumes, and you go to bed nearly everywhere within sound of running water – nature's ultimate soporific.

Even the wild animals behave with dignity and decorum in Banff National Park. Banff bears in no way resemble their alleged kinfolk in, say, Yellowstone. Yellowstone bears are overstuffed, revolting, moth-eaten panhandlers who snarl up traffic for miles while pursuing their gluttonous inclinations and make the night hideous by overturning garbage cans in search of snacks to ward off night starvation. Banff bears raid garbage cans too, but they lift the lids off very quietly. And they never hold up traffic. They prefer to walk at twilight along a forest path a few paces behind an unsuspecting tourist who is likely to lose a week's growth if he happens to turn around.

Banff bears have a sense of humour.

The chair-lift to the top of Mount Norquay carries one into regions of air otherwise inaccessible except to dyed-in-the-wool mountain-climbers; but the gondola to the top of Sulphur Mountain, a modest 8,000-foot hump overlooking the town-site, is a concession to modern softness. Such a contraption is morally permissible only to old-age pensioners and arthritics, but most of the customers appear under twenty-one and in sound health.

Lake Louise, forty miles west of Banff, is a place familiar to all Canadians and most Americans even though they have never visited it, for it is surely the most photographed beauty-spot on the continent and it looks exactly like its photographs. Word-pictures of the lake are almost as numerous and banal as the photographs, but one of the earliest, written by Rupert Brooke in 1913, has had some odd repercussions in our own time. A literature text-book adopted for use in Alberta schools a year or so ago included the Rupert Brooke description, but with one significant omission. Brooke's words – 'Banff is an ordinary little tourist resort in mountainous country, with hills and a stream and snow peaks beyond. Beautiful enough and invigorating. But Lake Louise – Lake Louise is of another world' – were made to read, 'Banff . . . is beautiful enough and invigorating.' The general editor of the text-book defended himself and his committee against the attacks of the purists on the grounds that Brooke's essay was badly dated and that the parts deleted 'didn't add [to] but detracted' from its value. He also pointed out that it is customary for editorial committees to delete 'offensive' passages from the plays of William Shakespeare.

The mountains surrounding Lake Louise are splendid to look at and uncomfortable to live with. Mountains, I feel, are unsuitable companions for the daily round. For they have nothing in common with temporal things – they belong among the most awesome symbols of eternity.

The best time to see the mountains of the West is at daybreak, not from within their shadow but from a point somewhere far out on the high plain. At first they seem to flow away into the distance in an unbroken mass, but as the dawn brightens they assume individual identity, separate into enormous hunch-backed figures, forever marching and forever fixed, that dwarf into nothingness all things that live; and the great plain in its uncomplicated immensity absorbs all traces of man's being. It is then, in the strange half-light of coming dawn, that the mountains and the plain assume a grandeur and immutability that compel the beholder, however arrogant he may be in the light of common day, to recognize his own insignificance.

I have often thought that the high plain and mountain country of Alberta is no place for an ambitious man. In the city you can build up and tear down skyscrapers and feel yourself a god; but no man can move a mountain or make more than a few scratches, soon to be obliterated, on the limitless surface of the plain.

The green mountain streams rush helter-skelter over rock and shale to join the waters of the Bow River – so to be borne east through the wide mountain valley and across the great plains into Lake Winnipeg and thence by the Nelson River into arctic seas. But the Highway points us in the opposite direction, towards the Great Divide, the height of land rising less than five miles beyond Lake Louise. Soon the land will fall away imperceptibly to the west and all the great rivers, no matter how wild and far their wanderings, flow at last into the Pacific.

Kicking Horse River at Field

The Epic Close

BRITISH COLUMBIA

'And what is so great', my wife said, 'about the Rogers Pass?'

'What is so great about the Rogers Pass', I said, 'is that we are over it.'

And that was true. The Rogers Pass, last link of the Trans-Canada Highway to be completed, built at a cost so astronomical that the figures fail to communicate any meaning, exists in the minds of those who have never seen it as a kind of Thermopylae where the mighty Selkirks make a last-ditch stand against the intrusive tourist, throw up great bastions he can surmount only on a series of hair-raising switch-backs, bombard him with rock-slides, avalanches — muster all the powers of hostile nature to sweep him from the face of the earth. In actual fact the Highway through the pass (lying within the boundaries of Glacier National Park, until 1962 accessible only by rail) is so superbly engineered that after the preceding stretch of up-and-down road from Field to Golden it comes as a distinct anti-climax. Here we were, my wife and I, lunching with fine appetite and light heart beside a burbling stream, hardly able to believe that we were up and over. We had encountered no dizzying switch-backs, dodged no falling rocks, peered into no bottomless abysses lying just beyond the Highway's edge. (These were to come later.) Mountains all around us, of course, close enough and high enough to occasion that slight constriction of the throat which always afflicts the plainsman when he can't see a hundred miles in every direction. But definitely not overpowering.

No doubt the Rogers Pass Highway was fantastically difficult to build but it is child's play for even the timidest tourist to drive.

One of the major problems involved in the construction of the

Rogers Pass

Highway through the Rogers Pass was avalanche control. The Trans-Canada Highway is designed as a year-round, all-weather road, and the Glacier National Park, where the Selkirks rise to over 10,000 feet, is notorious for the frequency and violence of its avalanches. The snowfall in the park averages thirty feet annually; in 1954 it reached fifty-four feet.

In 1956 when it was decided to abandon the old Big Bend route running north from Donald along the Columbia River and save 150 miles by cutting straight through Glacier Park from Donald to Revelstoke, an Avalanche Research Group made up of engineers, scientists from the National Research Council, and Swiss experts in snow-control established headquarters at Glacier in order to study snow conditions in the park and recommend ways of safeguarding the Highway against avalanches. Much of the work of the group was done on skis at high altitudes. The work was hard and often dangerous, but it paid off, and the Highway through the pass is now open all the year round.

Of the several methods adopted to protect the Highway from avalanches, the snowshed is the most obvious and effective. In Glacier more than half a mile of snowsheds, solidly built of steel and concrete and aesthetically pleasing when the light falls through the openings on the valley side, guard the most vulnerable spots. Other points are protected by cone-shaped mounds of earth up to twenty-five feet in height, against which the sliding snow piles up and usually swithers to a stop. Diverting dams, bench defences (dug-outs in the mountain sides up to 1,000 feet in length and 150 feet in width), and permanent gun emplacements are other control devices employed to ensure an open Highway. From the emplacements Canadian Army artillerymen lob mortar shells into areas of dangerous snow pile-up to start 'controlled' avalanches.

The scenery of Glacier National Park is wild, romantic, and so far almost wholly uncorrupted by evidences of man's presence. Until 1962 it was the preserve of the few, mostly mountain-climbers — now for the first time it is open to every human being who owns a car or a bicycle, and it is a question how long the park will be able to keep itself unspotted from the world. Fortunately it is difficult to deface mountains.

Beyond the Rogers Pass the Highway follows a narrow, high-walled valley to Revelstoke, a town laid out in neat squares on the flats of the Columbia River and celebrated for its heavy snowfall and splendid skiing facilities. We did not linger in Revelstoke, nor did we take the mountain road to Revelstoke National Park which sits atop a mountain 6,000 feet up and no doubt commands a fine view of the surrounding landscape. The truth is that by the time we reached Revelstoke my wife and I were both suffering acutely from the claustrophobia that sustained travel through high, closed-in places often induces in prairie-dwellers; and at Revelstoke there seemed hardly space enough to allow a man to turn around without rubbing off some skin on a mountain-side. We therefore accepted on faith the assurances of the local tourist bureau that Revelstoke is a sportsman's paradise and continued our way through the pinched and constricting valley. Forty-five miles west of Revelstoke, Little Shuswap Lake comes into view — a marvellous expanse of sky-blue water flanked by great hills which stand back far enough from the water's edge to allow room for wide sand beaches – and it is possible to breathe freely again.

We liked Salmon Arm, a town scattered casually up and down hill-sides overlooking the western end of Little Shuswap. We swam in the lake, sun-bathed on a beach backed by stately fir trees and lofty hills, and in the evening walked for miles through the upper reaches of the town and among the orchards and dairy farms on the outskirts. No one in Salmon Arm appears to have heard of town planning. There is a town centre where streets and buildings conform to a more or less orthodox pattern, but the residential streets and suburbs wander indiscriminately up and down hill-sides, disappear completely for no apparent reason, and pop up again on hill-tops and in forest-clearings. There are orchards everywhere, for Salmon Arm marks the northern extremity of the great Okanagan Valley fruit-belt. Some of the orchards have been allowed to run wild, giving the countryside a dishevelled look, and even in the best residential districts of the town the lawns and shrubs look a bit unkempt. Elsewhere in Canada we diligently prune our shrubs and clip our hedges and shave our lawns and compete for prizes offered by the service clubs for the best-groomed yard or block; but most British Columbia towns we passed through shared Salmon Arm's slightly ragged look. 'Things grow so fast here we can't keep up,' one Salmon Arm citizen informed us. 'I get the lawn slick as a pool-table one day and she's running wild the next. Discouraging – that's what it is.'

He didn't look discouraged, he looked contented and well preserved, and I suspect that his lawn-mower – if he owned one – was in the garage gathering rust. The truth is that outside the industrial towns, life in British Columbia is so pleasant that it seems absurd to waste any part of it trying to improve on nature. It is much more sensible to spend one's leisure time in the manner of our Salmon Arm informant – sitting on the front lawn under an umbrella-shade watching the pretty girls trip by.

From our motel porch we saw a Salmon Arm ancient, a brown, wrinkled, white-haired old man, stride down the Highway towards the town two miles below in the valley. He wore tattered carpet-slippers and carried a pair of boots that looked as old as himself. He returned some time later at a speed of about four miles an hour (up-hill), wearing the boots and carrying the carpet-slippers.

To those of us who in our ignorance assume that all of British Columbia is green and lush and smothered from end to end by fruits of the earth our first sight of the 'interior' comes as a distinct shock. The interior of British Columbia, which the Highway enters through the valley of the South Thompson River, is a wild, semi-arid, techni-coloured land of rolling, sun-burned hills, wide river-valleys, deep craggy canyons, sagebrush, and stunted ponderosa pine. In many ways it bears a striking resemblance to the desert country of the American south-west. Successful farming is possible only in irrigated districts; the rest of the interior is largely given over to ranching.

The town of Kamloops, at the junction of the North and South Thompson rivers, has some things to commend it, including an admirable scenic location and a lengthy history. David Stuart, a trader with John Jacob Astor's Pacific Fur Company, built the original Fort Kamloops in 1812. The following year the Pacific and North West companies merged, and in 1821 were absorbed by the Hudson's Bay Company. Fort Kamloops was thus an important fur-trading centre long before any of the coastal cities was founded. Later it enjoyed a brief flurry of excitement during the mid-century gold-rush days, before settling down to middle-aged respectability.

It is one of the pleasant ironies of history, and cause of hope for all of us, that it is possible for a man to achieve great reputation and even enduring fame by doing something just a little worse than any-one else. Thirty-odd years ago an otherwise undistinguished football player stole every headline in the American newspapers and wrote his name large in the annals of football by running seventy yards the wrong way in a Rose Bowl game. Captain Scott and his companions lost their race to reach the South Pole and died; and in losing and dying gained a kind of earthly immortality denied their superbly efficient and successful rival, Roald Amundsen. And the beautiful Donner Pass through the High Sierras of California between Sacramento and Lake Tahoe honours the names and memories of a tragically incompetent party of emigrants many of whom perished miserably in the pass when trapped by snow.

These meditations were prompted by recollections of the almost unbelievable trek of a party of tenderfoot gold-seekers across the prairies and through the great mountains to Kamloops in the year 1862. The original Overlanders, as the trekkers were known, were Old Country men who succumbed to the lures of an early travel agency, the Overland Transit Company. For the modest sum of £42 the company offered transportation from London to the western plains, from whence – so prospective emigrants were assured – it would be an easy journey by stage-coach across the plains and through the Yellowhead Pass 250 miles west of Fort Edmonton to the headwaters of the Fraser, the great river of gold. And once on the Fraser it would of course be mere child's play to build rafts from the abundant standing timber and float gently down the river to the gold-fields proper.

The original Overlanders from England, relatively few in number, were joined by many eager gold-seekers from eastern Canada. They all reached St. Paul, Minnesota, the end of steel, without difficulty. There they found that they were on their own, the transit company having made no provision for further transport. A few of the Overlanders turned back, but most of them made their way by ox-cart, steamboat, and foot to Fort Garry. At the Fort they bought Red River carts and loaded them with pemmican; and in small, surprisingly well-organized and strictly disciplined parties they set off across the plains towards the mountains lying nearly a thousand miles to the west. The first party of Overlanders reached Fort Edmonton towards the end of July; the last, several weeks later. From Fort Edmonton they travelled straight west, hacked and clawed their way through dense forest along the banks of the Athabasca River, crossed the Yellowhead Pass, built rafts, and floated, waded, and swam down and through the tumultuous waters of one of the wildest streams on earth to Quesnel and the gold-fields.

One group of thirty-odd, including a pregnant woman and three small children, made their way by raft and on foot down the North Thompson. When they reached Kamloops the pregnant woman was in labour. The next day she gave birth to Rose Schubert, the first white child born in the interior of British Columbia.

It is easy to summarize the achievement of the Overlanders and almost impossible to believe it. They endured hardships without compare in the history of western Canadian settlement; their rafts were wrecked time and again in the mad waters of the Fraser and the North Thompson; they portaged for miles through otherwise impassable canyons; they lost most of their supplies and they ate their livestock. Some of the Overlanders drowned and a few may have starved to death but most of them reached their El Dorado only to find that the gold-fields had petered out. Some returned to the East, the rest faded quietly into the prosaic background of the ordinary, unglamorous, workaday world as farmers, mill-hands, lumbermen, shop-keepers, bartenders, whose names are now mostly forgotten.

Had the Overlanders died to the last man somewhere along the trail their story would be everywhere known and their memory green. But because they refused to leave their bones to bleach in a mountain pass they will never be more than an insignificant fragment of the great epic of Western settlement. By staying alive they missed becoming part of the legend of the centuries.

West of Kamloops the country becomes progressively more arid. Kamloops Lake, a magnificent stretch of water twenty miles long, does much to modify the desert aspect of the surrounding terrain; and the village of Savona at the west end of the lake brings to mind an obscure item of local history. In 1885 the village was renamed Van Horne in honour of the great railroad-builder, and Van Horne it remained until Sir William actually saw the huddle of shacks to

which he had lent his name — whereupon he insisted that the village take back the old one.

The loneliest places of earth are not those where man has never set foot but those from which he has withdrawn defeated, leaving behind him a few pathetic evidences of his presence and his dream. An abandoned mining town is far lonelier than a great sand desert, a tumble-down farmstead than a stretch of virgin prairie. Wallachin, now hardly more than a name printed minutely on a map, but once the centre of a flourishing agricultural community, lies just off the Trans-Canada Highway about halfway between Savona and Ashcroft. Here the valley of the Thompson is wide and spectacularly beautiful; lonely not because it is empty of life but because a few ragged, sterile apple-trees standing in line across a sun-baked field where nothing else grows, and a few pieces of rotten flume clinging to the hill-sides remind us that less than half a century ago men lived and worked here and made of Wallachin one of the show-places of the interior of British Columbia.

Lived, some of them, to see the work of years vanish almost overnight.

The area was developed by a promotional company early in the century. The land was cultivated and planted largely to apple-trees, water was brought in through wooden flumes running along hill-sides and across gullies for twenty miles or more, and within a decade Wallachin was the centre of a flourishing community, mostly Old Country, presided over by the Marquess of Anglesey who built a fine mansion complete with swimming-pool on a point overlooking the river. But the enterprise collapsed with shocking suddenness. On the outbreak of the First World War in 1914 nearly all the able-bodied men of the district went off to fight; a year or two later large sections of the flume were swept away in a cloud-burst and there was not sufficient man-power left to repair the damage; blight struck the apple-trees; financial backers of the original enterprise refused to invest more money; and within another ten years the desert of brown, withered grass and sagebrush had again taken over, leaving only a few scraggly apple-trees to survive as melancholy reminders of fair hopes now blasted.

Near Cache Creek the Thompson makes a right-angle turn and flows almost straight south, parallel with the coastal ranges, to its junction with the Fraser at Lytton. The Highway follows the river through a valley which presently contracts into a canyon; and it is now rather than in the great mountain passes lying far to the east that the ordinary motorist with an ordinary nervous system may begin to feel the sweat-beads gathering on his forehead. The Highway is wide and admirably engineered, but the canyon floor at times lies far, far below and there is almost sure to be construction going on somewhere which occasionally forces the driver to an outside edge where there seems to be distressingly little space between himself and eternity. The canyon itself is dry and sun-baked but seldom constricting, and the river is an ice-green, white-flecked thread lying seemingly immobile between yellow rock-walls. Occasionally a toy train appears down near the water's edge and slides snake-like into a barely visible hole which is the entrance to a tunnel; and far to the west the great mountains of the coastal ranges pile up in disordered masses.

Ashcroft, lying just off the Highway near the point where the Thompson turns south, was a well-known supply depot and jumping-off place for the gold-fields in the days of the gold-rush, but perhaps it will be longest remembered as the centre of a colony of county English, determined, like so many similar colonies, to maintain Old Country social institutions and customs in the middle of an untamed wilderness. Around the colony there has accumulated inevitably a body of legend which no doubt contains the essence if not the detail of truth; and of all the legends told and retold about the Ashcroft Englishmen the most widely known is that of riding to hounds.

The Cornwall brothers, avid huntsmen who represented the squirearchy in the colony, imported from England a pack of fox-hounds and democratically invited the local cowboys to join them and their fellow Englishmen in the first fox-hunt of the season, on the understanding that the etiquette of the hunt be at all times rigidly observed. The cowboys, pleased to be invited to share in the fun, gave solemn assurances of polite behaviour and agreed to join their hosts in shouting 'Tally-ho' and 'Gone away' at the appropriate times. Unfortunately, when the hounds raised a fox (actually a coyote, for there were no foxes in the Ashcroft country) conditioning triumphed over intention. With mighty yells of 'There goes the son of a bitch!' the cowboys thundered off across the sun-baked flats, overran the hounds, and lassoed the coyote.

Whereupon the Englishmen laid away their pink coats and never put them on again.

The canyon of the Fraser River is a wonder and a horror – a nightmarish crack in the earth between 3,000-foot walls through which runs the most ferocious river in all Canada – a dirty, fighting, snarling, wildcat river desperate to escape the great rock-walls, which, pressed by the tumbled mountains of the coast range, in turn press in on the river, force it at times through channels so narrow that its depth is doubled and even tripled. (At Hell's Gate the river is 120 feet wide and sometimes 180 feet deep.) It breaks from the canyon exhausted, and in a kind of surly disgust spews forth its silt to form the great delta on which the cities of New Westminster and Vancouver now stand.

The Thompson canyon is often wide; it is rich in colour and the river is a bright green band drawn against an ochre background. The Fraser Canyon is narrow and dark and the river a brown, swirling tide. Travellers unfamiliar with the canyon never really see it – only experience teaches you where to stop for the occasional rare vista which the seventy-mile run affords. The view from the summit of Jackass Mountain, twelve miles south of Lytton, is one of the best. The Trans-Canada Highway at times follows the upper rim of the canyon, at times drops down to run along the great rock-face on the eastern side; and near the canyon's end it crosses the river from east to west, but the view from the middle of the bridge is sadly constricted by the bends in the canyon-wall. Only those defeated by life and eager to return to the womb could possibly feel at ease in the canyon of the Fraser.

We found the canyon a frightening, sinister place, and to add to our discomfiture the road was under construction in several places and more than once we were forced to the outside edge of a built-up detour that crept around a projecting corner of rock. One

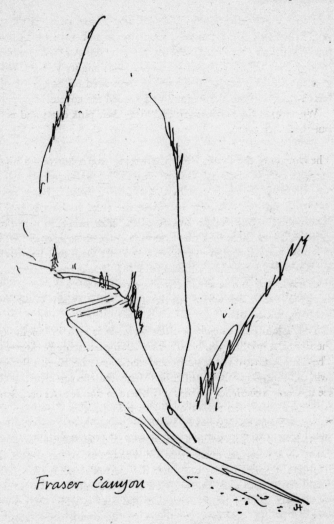

Fraser Canyon

thing we saw that raised our spirits remarkably – a sign at a point where the road clung to the side of the canyon, sheer rock-walls above and below, warning us to look out for livestock on the Highway. So far as we could see, livestock could reach the road only by falling from the pasture land on the rim hundreds of feet above our heads.

Alexander Mackenzie was the first white man to see the Fraser River. On his journey in 1792-3 in search of the western ocean he crossed from the headwaters of the Peace to the Fraser, entered the waters of the Fraser near the point where the city of Prince George now stands, ran the stream south for a hundred miles, then, dismayed by the ferocity of the currents and the numerous rapids, abandoned the river and made his way west through the coastal mountains and down the Bella Coola to the Pacific.

Simon Fraser, like Mackenzie a partner in the North West Company, undertook to complete the exploration of the river which Mackenzie had begun. On May 22nd, 1808, he set out from Fort George (now Prince George) on the maddest of all Western journeys of exploration, in four canoes carrying twenty-four men. Five weeks later he reached the Pacific, having made the entire journey by the river to which he gave his name.

Five weeks of hell. The men were harassed constantly by hostile Indians; they were forced to abandon their canoes above the narrow gap later called Hell's Gate; they scrambled on foot over wet, slippery rocks, crawled along cliff-faces on webs of ladders fashioned by the Indians, but somehow came through without a single casualty. Fraser describes the passage of Hell's Gate in flat, prosaic terms which, as anyone who has ever seen Hell's Gate realizes, constitute a miracle of understatement:

'We had to pass where no human beings should venture. . . . Steps which are formed like a ladder on the shrouds of a ship; long poles hanging to one another and crossed at certain distances with twigs, the whole suspended from the top to the foot of the deep precipices and fastened at both extremities to stones and trees, furnish a safe and convenient passage to the natives; but we, who had not the advantage of their education and experience, were often in imminent danger when obliged to follow their example.'

History redeems the dark and dismal canyon and gives it life. Heroic men and foolish men passed through its narrow confines; and here more than a century ago they worked and fought for gold, for the Fraser River showed the way to the gold-fields far to the north by laying the bait within comparatively tranquil waters around Hope and Yale.

The real gold-fields – Quesnel, Antler Creek, Williams Creek, Barkerville – lay hundreds of miles up the Fraser, far beyond the northern limits of the canyon; but such were the fearful difficulties of terrain created by the north-south run of coastal ranges that for the gold-hunters pouring into the colony of British Columbia by sea from eastern Canada, the United States, and far-off places of the Empire, the Fraser provided the only possible route to follow. Steamboats – if they didn't blow up – carried the miners up-stream as far as Yale. From that point on, the journey to the gold-fields was made eventually over the most famous road in the West – the Cariboo Trail.

The Cariboo Trail was Sir James Douglas's most extravagant large-scale experiment in road-building, and the most visionary. The surveying of the road and some of the actual construction were done by a detachment of Royal Engineers sent out from England by Sir Edward Bulwer-Lytton, Colonial Secretary and one-time popular novelist, to maintain order in the far-west colony and 'develop institutes of civilization'. The institute of civilization of greatest interest to Sir James Douglas was a road which, so he dreamed, would immediately provide transport to the interior and some day link British Columbia with the rest of Canada. The road to the gold-fields which the excellent Engineers surveyed and in part built continued in use until the coming of the C.P.R. in 1885. The Cariboo Trail is beyond question the most remarkable road-building achievement in our history, running as it did almost the full length of the Fraser River canyon and to Barkerville 250 miles beyond.

The gold-fields of the Cariboo, long since played out, lie far north of the Trans-Canada Highway, but it is possible when driving through the Fraser River canyon to feel something of the spirit of that far-off time when men placer-mined the sandbars and creeks of the canyon, when steamboats plied furiously between Yale and the river mouth, and when men and horses moved to and from the gold-fields along the trail which, like today's Trans-Canada Highway, crept along the canyon-walls. And it is comforting to know that, although the old Cariboo Trail was much narrower than the Trans-Canada Highway and without guard-rails, surprisingly few men fell off it into the river.

Below Hope the river widens and begins its western swing towards Vancouver and the Pacific, 100 miles away. It runs now through what is called the valley of the Fraser as distinct from the canyon, in reality a delta of rich black earth which the river has created over aeons of time. We have, I feel, a right to expect a stream to emerge from the mountains gay and sparkling and crystal clear. Most streams do. But not the Fraser. It is no longer a savage, snarling torrent but it is sullen and dirty to the end. The valley itself is beautiful, intensively cultivated, rich in market gardens and small fruits and dairy herds and hay-fields. One of its chief delights is the sense of freedom it communicates by contrast. We who have been long immured in the dark canyon suddenly find it possible to lift up our eyes and see something other than a wall of rock, to breathe deeply again without fear of starting an avalanche. The air is heavy with the mingled scent of new-mown hay and many flowers and the occasional discordant whiff of fertilizer; and the mountains on either side – those to the south in the state of Washington dominated by Mount Baker, its cone-shaped summit eternally snow-clad – sit back and discreetly solicit our attention rather than force themselves upon us.

As the Highway nears the great cities at the river's end, dairy herds become the most characteristic feature of the landscape, for the valley of the Fraser supplies Vancouver with its milk. They provide a charming pastoral touch to delight the heart of the innocent traveller who has never milked a cow by hand, never been slapped across the face by a heavy tail, never had a bucket of milk kicked into his lap. I grant that a dairy cow standing knee-deep in grass under a spreading oak or maple creates a pleasing picture, but to myself and the ex-farmboys of my generation she will always be a symbol of serfdom; for no matter where we were or what exciting things we were doing we had always to be home at a certain hour to milk the stupid, cud-chewing tyrants who, so it seemed to us, dictated the very pattern of our lives.

There is much to do and see and marvel at in Vancouver. The shops are numerous and large, the crowds exciting, and musical and night-club entertainment available, and in the fall the Pacific National Exhibition plays host to all who have the mind and energy for such things. Vancouver's streets are wider than those of most Canadian cities, her parks more luxuriant and numerous, her gardens a glory not only in the summer but nearly all the year round, her Chinatown the largest in Canada. And in the background the Lions Gate Bridge hangs like a modified rainbow arch over the narrow entrance to the great harbour.

Vancouver is a port city. Port cities possess an enormous advantage over those built inland, for the combination of sea and land is inevitably more varied and interesting than either by itself; and for all men the sea holds the attraction of the mysterious and unknown. A port city acquires glamour merely through the presence of ships in its harbour, for a ship is of man-made things inherently the most romantic. All devices of transport, even the creaking Red River cart, are romantic because they are invested with some hint of the magic of distance. But the ship is one of the oldest of such devices; it is the most graceful and except for the airplane goes the farthest. The airplane offers no competition because it is a Johnny-come-lately without a history to match against that brought instantly to mind by mention of such names as the *Santa Maria*, the *Golden Hind*, the *Mayflower*, the *Erebus*, and the *Terror*, or of the unnamed curragh in which St. Brendan crossed the Atlantic — as all right-thinking Irishmen agree — and discovered America a thousand years before Columbus.

Has earth anything to show more fair than a great ship standing out to sea or a dirty coaster butting down a channel on a mad March day? A railway train can sometimes stir emotions similar to those which a ship excites, but only in the hearts of those of us who grew up a long time ago in some lonely place where the train was our one connecting link with the great world lying somewhere beyond the limit of our mean horizons. Then the most magical sight our eyes beheld was a row of lights moving through the dark night to the accompaniment of the most haunting sound on earth, the whistle of a steam-engine — by comparison with which the curious emission of a contemporary diesel is a thing to laugh at. Or weep over.

Vancouver has a harbour and it has Stanley Park — a thousand acres of forest primeval within walking distance of the city's heart. The park is worth cherishing, not only as a place of beauty and quiet adjacent to the madhouse which is any modern industrial city, but as a vital link with the past, for all Vancouver was once very much like Stanley Park — though considerably less well-groomed — and the splendid Douglas firs make of history a living thing and remind us of the herculean labours of the builders of the city.

A promenade backed by the great firs runs along English Bay and skirts the park. Elderly ladies and gentlemen impeccably dressed in costumes vaguely reminiscent of Edwardian days stroll along the promenade morning and afternoon, and invalids and the very old from rest-homes near by sit in wheel-chairs and stare with dim eyes at the ships in the bay; and behind them the Douglas firs rise dark and majestic and the worlds of modern sheltered urban man and axe-wielding pioneer reach across a century of time and touch one another.

It is a discouraging and fearful thought — likely to strike anyone looking at Vancouver's ever-changing skyline — that there is not, nor can there be, much that is permanent about a modern city. We may praise this or that building, applaud an ingenious and seemingly far-sighted piece of town planning, but always in the knowledge that what we praise today may all be swept away tomorrow. What, after all, is left of the Toronto or Montreal of a hundred years ago? Our Canadian cities have been founded too late in time and built of the wrong stuff to ensure them any sort of permanence. Perhaps the only part of a Canadian city worth talking about is its setting, or at least such parts of its setting as seem likely to be preserved for posterity.

Vancouver is in some respects a monstrous creation. It has grown far too fast to permit proper planning and it already blights areas of extraordinary beauty that should have been left untouched. It is a

city that should have grown straight up, like Manhattan, instead
of despoiling great mountain-sides and blotching fair valleys. But
a view over the city from some high point just at sunset, after a stiff
breeze has blown away the smog, silences criticism. Whatever claims
to our admiration Vancouver may establish must be in terms not
of streets and skyscrapers and shopping centres, but of the firs in
Stanley Park and the mountains and the sea and the great ships
coming in to harbour from far-off places. The part of Vancouver
that is enduring – not her buildings nor her industries nor her
people – is beyond praise or blame because it is no work of man.

We sailed from Vancouver on a day of flawless beauty aboard a
C.P.R. ferry-boat bound for Vancouver Island. The water was pure
sapphire, the sky cloudless, the wind a mere breath on the face.
We had made the crossing twice before, both times in a near gale
on a grey day, and today was a revelation. We had never really
seen the city. Above all we had never really seen the islands of the
Gulf of Georgia.

To our left on Point Grey the University of British Columbia
crept into view, a hodge-podge of buildings tumbled down indiscriminately on the most beautiful campus on the continent. The city
thrust out tentative feelers, straggled for a few miles along the coast,
and then petered out. To the north Howe Sound, for a time cut off
from view by interlocking islands, opened up its magnificent thirty-
mile reach. In the background great mountains, invisible from the
shore, pushed their snow-clad peaks against the sky. And everywhere ships. Dredges, pleasure boats, fishing smacks, tugs pushing
great lumber rafts, freighters nosing in and out among the islands,
a rival ferry heading like ourselves for Nanaimo, and a great
P. & O. liner – the glorious white-winged *Oriana* – outward bound
for the Orient.

The islands of the gulf hang suspended between sky and ocean,
shrouded in a blue haze that distorts objects, blots out all precise
lines, creates impressionistic landscapes. The islands are nearly all
inhabited, and no wonder. Some of the inhabitants are normal
people like you and me, and some, so rumour tells, are strange
creatures who sleep when they are sleepy, eat when they are hungry,
and in between times toil not, neither spin, but fish and read and

meditate in the sun. Meditate with blue sky above and a blue sea in front, a sea which in quiet weather appears tideless, without a ripple, without a wrinkle, the surface broken only by the wake of a passing ship or the spray cast up by a plunging gannet. And beyond on the mainland the mountains form a supremely dramatic backdrop, summits wreathed in snow, bases shrouded in palls of smoke which mark the dwelling-places of poor fools whose lives are regulated by clocks and lunch hours and sermons and Home and School meetings and fun on Saturday night. It is surely a sad commentary on the human condition that we brand as eccentrics men and women who do what they want to do. The rest of us, the huge submerged majority who do not live on the Gulf Islands, can do little more than echo the cry of our archetype, George F. Babbitt — 'Practically, I've never done a single thing I've wanted to in my whole life!'

The ferry decants its passengers at Nanaimo, a bustling little town with a harbour full of fishing boats, set among rolling hills and wearing that slightly tousled look characteristic of nearly all British Columbia towns and particularly those of Vancouver Island. Luxuriant growth has sometimes awkward consequences; on Vancouver Island you feel that if you relax your vigilance for a moment — and the temptation to relax not just for a moment but permanently is hard to resist — you will wake up some morning to find your lawn overrun by towering Douglas firs.

The run from Nanaimo to Victoria, about seventy miles over the splendid new Trans-Canada Highway, unfortunately passes most of the way through heavy forest. Sea vistas are few; and my wife and I preferred to cover a good part of the distance poking along the old highway which follows the coast much more closely than the new, and leads through some delightful sea-shore towns including Cowichan, famous for the sweaters which the Hudson's Bay Company taught the Indians to knit.

Duncan, lying just off the Highway midway between Nanaimo and Victoria, is reputed to be populated almost entirely by eccentric Englishmen. Undoubtedly the town has in its time enjoyed its full share of younger sons, remittance men, retired rear-admirals, major-generals, and gentleman farmers who left the cows unmilked in order to finish a cricket match or a set of tennis. But what, after all, is so eccentric about leaving a cow unmilked in order to finish a cricket match? What is foolishness to the Greeks is gospel to the enlightened. Certainly Vancouver Island is a world in which men from the mainland frequently acquire a brand new set of values. That the rest of Canada is hard-working and virtuous is no reason why the citizens of Duncan and similar communities should be denied their cakes and ale. Thus they reason and thus they live.

The Malahat Drive begins about twenty miles north of Victoria and extends to the outskirts of the city. The Highway runs through heavily wooded country and explores a fine canyon. It provides a look-out point halfway along the Drive which, if it weren't for the obstructive smoke-clouds belched from the chimney of a cement plant on the sea-shore far below, would command the handsomest readily accessible view along the entire length of the Highway: a superb, island-dotted seascape, small boats and ferries plying the dark blue foreground waters, the mountains of the mainland breaking the far-distant skyline, and − detached, aloof, Olympian − the white peak of Mount Baker a hundred miles to the east, suspended like a cone-shaped cloud in a great void.

The city of Victoria has perpetrated the most successful hoax in the history of tourism − it has persuaded the rest of the world that it is indeed a little bit of old England. Perhaps there was some warrant for the view half a century ago but there is none now. Victoria has of course rather more than its share of tweedy old gentlemen and even tweedier ladies who haunt mausoleums like the Empress Hotel and the Union Club where tea and port are drunk in silence and the click of a billiard ball shatters the eardrums; but a day or two in the city is surely all that is needed to convince those of us of clear eye and level head that we are being exposed to a wonderfully entertaining − and for the city wonderfully profitable − piece of stagecraft.

Victoria is not England; she has simply played on her origins to give the tourist what he wants. Nowhere in England will you find a city remotely resembling Victoria, for Victoria is self-consciously and deliberately Old Country, hence not Old Country at all. And once the contradiction is uncovered the real nature of the city becomes clear.

Victoria belongs properly in Disneyland. Anyone doubting this statement should visit the replica of Anne Hathaway's Cottage standing cheek-by-jowl with the Old Curiosity Shop in – so help us God – Chaucer Lane. When my wife and I visited the lane, Chaucer and Dickens were nowhere in sight – off eating crumpets with Anne Hathaway no doubt – but a London bobby faultlessly attired in blue uniform and helmet took us in charge and tried to sell us tickets to the Old Curiosity Shop. He seemed hurt when we said we were just looking.

The best way to arrive in Victoria is by boat, for the harbour is virtually the city's heart. The Empress Hotel and its fine gardens, and the Legislative Buildings – no more or less inspired than the general run of provincial legislative buildings – flank the harbour, and after you have drunk tea in the hotel and made a pious pilgrimage to the parliament grounds to look at the memorial to Sir James Douglas, first governor of British Columbia and our most visionary road-builder, there is really nothing more to see or do in Victoria. There are of course innumerable marvels to which the tourist bureau brochures direct our attention – Craigdarroch Castle, Dominion Observatory, Royal Roads, and a hundred more – but the truth is that once the initial shock has worn off, once we have adjusted to the idea that 'quaintness' can be cultivated to the immense profit of the cultivators, Victoria, like nearly all our cities, becomes significant only in relation to its setting.

About that setting Rudyard Kipling said the final word more than half a century ago:

'To realize Victoria you must take all that the eye admires most in Bournemouth, Torquay, the Isle of Wight, the Happy Valley at Hong Kong, the Doon, Sorrento, and Camps Bay; add reminiscences of the Thousand Islands and arrange the whole round the Bay of Naples, with some Himalayas for background.

'Real estate agents recommend it as a little piece of England . . . but no England is set in such seas or so fully charged with the mystery of the larger ocean beyond. The high, still twilights along the beaches are out of the old East just under the curve of the world, and even in October the sun rises warm from the first. Earth, sky and water wait outside every man's door to drag him out to play if he looks up from his work; and though some other cities in the Dominion do not quite understand this immoral mood of Nature, men who have made their money in them go off to Victoria and with the zeal of converts preach and preserve its beauties.'

For my wife and me, journey's end was a motel shaded by great evergreens on the outskirts of Victoria, where under the evergreens or in deck-chairs beside the swimming-pool we relaxed and absorbed the sunshine and thought of all the people we should talk to, the sights we should see, the things we should do, and dismissed them all from our minds as irrelevant and inconsequential. Victoria is no place for an energetic man – he should live in Vancouver or Calgary or Winnipeg or Toronto or Montreal. But at least, in the course of our musings on all the things we would not do in Victoria, we hit upon the answer to a question which has for long vexed many earnest people – why are religious sects so numerous and so lively on Vancouver Island? The answer is really very simple. Life on Vancouver Island and throughout the entire gulf region is so pleasant, so well worth living, and so easy to live that the inhabitants are naturally anxious for some sort of assurance that it will continue forever. (For those of us who endure the rigours of life in a place like Saskatchewan the assurance is of less importance.)

No doubt lovers of the dramatic feel that the Trans-Canada Highway should end at some high point overlooking the city of Vancouver where the beauty of the land and its booming industrial life are both to be seen at their most spectacular. But for those of us who have travelled the Highway from ocean to ocean and have come to look upon it as an epic (in asphalt) Victoria provides the perfect ending. For your true epic moves to a serene and quiet close – as in Homer, Virgil, and Milton – and Victoria is quiet as the tomb.

The golden twilight comes and Mount Baker fades beyond sight. Night falls, and the air is soft and warm and flower-scented. The images of day recede, peace comes dropping slow, and I am convinced that had the ancients who dreamed of the Blessed Isles lying far to the west – and in some instances spent their lives searching for them – ever reached Victoria and the islands of the gulf they would have been content to search no farther.

The Tie That Binds?

It was the dream of Sir James Douglas and is still the hope of all Canadians to whom national unity is a passionately desired end that a trans-Canada highway should draw closer together all parts of the nation and help us, if not to love, at least to understand one another. 'This event has generated a renewed sense of national unity,' Prime Minister John Diefenbaker said in declaring the Highway open. 'It has brought about a sense of oneness from the Atlantic to the Pacific Ocean comparable to that which moved Canadians when the first Canadian transcontinental railway was completed. . . . It is a day when another landmark is met and passed in the building of a strong Canadianism.'

These are brave words and, let us hope, prophetic; but it needs more than a highway to create a sense of oneness in a nation. Familiarity sometimes breeds affection – and sometimes indifference or contempt. (Ontario and Quebec have always enjoyed ready access to one another.) But travelling the length of the Trans-Canada Highway is in one sense at least a salutary experience – it makes us aware of the peculiar physical structure of our country and the problems arising therefrom. In this awareness it is possible that understanding of one another may begin.

The Highway at no time runs more than 200 miles above the border between Canada and the United States, and yet for much of the 5,000-mile drive the traveller experiences the sensation, and legitimately so, of being on the northern fringes of civilization with not much between him and the North Pole except forest and tundra and arctic seas. To travel the length of the Highway is to see Canada not as it looks on the map (a vast land area of almost equal length and breadth) but as a strip of land 5,000 miles long and from 100 to 400 miles wide, compressed between one of the most populous nations on earth and a northern waste.

The physical barriers between geographical regions are real and sometimes terrifying. Nearly 100 miles of ocean lies between New-foundland and the rest of the country. Prince Edward Island too is cut off from the mainland; and so, except for the narrowest of connecting links, is Nova Scotia. Between central Ontario and the prairie provinces lies a thousand miles of lake and rock and tree, much of it an impenetrable wilderness. There are cleared areas along the Highway through the Laurentian Shield, and a few substantial towns, but they represent no continuous line of settlement. This is raw, barbarous country in which it is foolish to stray far from the Highway, for the wilderness lies all about you and it is reluctant to yield up those who commit themselves in ignorance to its keeping. 'The Highway is neither built nor intended as an expressway, nor does it generally pass through areas of mass population,' says the Canadian Government Travel Bureau in what is surely a classic example of unintentional understatement.

West of the prairies rise the great mountains. They isolate British Columbia, compel her to turn her back on the rest of Canada. British Columbia faces south and west. Central Canada faces south. The Maritimes face south and east. The physical structure of our country forbids us to look to a common centre.

For a long time now we Canadians have been much concerned about establishing a national identity, projecting an image which will satisfy ourselves and impress favourably the rest of the world. We are tired of being looked upon as a rather colourless people who will all eventually slip into heaven for no other reason than that we lack courage to be damned. Many reasons have been advanced to explain our comparative failure to realize that distinctive identity; but no one, unless he has travelled the Trans-Canada Highway, can fully understand the degree to which our physical environment inhibits its emergence.

Some years ago a distinguished critic of Canadian culture charged that Canadian painting represented a clear case of arrested development. Since our society is now largely urban, he said, our

painters should be painting people. Instead they can still be found —
like the Group of Seven before them — painting large chunks of the
Laurentian Shield. But anyone driving the Trans-Canada Highway
through Ontario, either by No. 17 along the north shore of Lake
Superior or by No. 11 over the top through Cochrane and Hearst,
will understand that this continuing compulsion to go on painting
the Laurentian Shield involves much more than mere imitation of
a once-popular school. It is a measure of the extent to which we
are still under the domination of a physical environment so vast, so
overwhelming, that only in one or two crowded cities can we hope
to escape its impact. Drive the Highway from coast to coast — much
of the distance through dense, silent, oppressive forest — and you
are aware, every mile you drive, that less than a day's journey north
begins one of the last great wildernesses of earth, a wilderness which
dwarfs into utter insignificance the narrow band of settlement,
itself far from continuous, running from ocean to ocean.

Herein may lie the real explanation of our failure thus far to
develop that positive aggressive personality our national advertising
men yearn for. We are a people subconsciously aware of the gods,
of mighty immanent forces that compel us to acknowledge, however reluctantly, our own inconsequence.

To travel the Trans-Canada Highway for its full length is an
exhilarating and exhausting experience best enjoyed, as most travel
on the North American continent is, in the early spring or fall when
the weather is temperate, the blackflies and mosquitoes quiescent,
and the traffic light. Along the way lies much of the finest scenery
our country has to offer; and the trails and waterways and places
where men lived long ago, to which the Highway leads us, have
power — if our imaginations are not completely stultified — to bring
the past to life and people it with grand *seigneurs* and *coureurs de
bois* and tough, single-minded loyalists and fanatic gold-miners and
red-coated Mounties and all the splendid host of ordinary home-
spun men and women who cleared and tilled the land and in due
season gave their bodies to it. And those of us who cherish such
simple yet rarely realized joys as silence and solitude and the peace
that comes through separation from the ways of men can easily find

them – often along the Highway itself and never more than an hour's drive away.

The Trans-Canada Highway is an engineering, communications, and scenic marvel, and the traveller who follows its path from St. John's to Victoria is no doubt justified in feeling that he has added much to his knowledge of places and people. But perhaps the ultimate knowledge the Highway brings to those who travel it is – paradoxically – that marvels cannot permanently satisfy the human heart. No matter how exalted we may be for a time by movement and change, by snow-crowned mountains and wide empty spaces and the tumbled chaos of rock and lake and forest and the tumultuous surging life of great cities, we weary sooner or later of the Highway. We leave the long straight line flanked by wonders that astonish the eye and uplift the spirit for the narrow circle that in the end calls the wanderer home – the circle of intimate human associations which, however limited, alone justify the experience of living.